W9-ATO-185

OIL CITY LIBRARY
2 Central Avenue • Oil City, PA 16301

In Memory of

Donald W. Schwitzer

Presented by

Oil City Aerie #283
Fraternal Order of Eagles

Whitetail

Behavior Through The Seasons

Text and photography by

Charles J. Alsheimer.

G599.652
AL78w

OIL CITY LIBRARY
2 CENTRAL AVENUE
OIL CITY, PA. 16301

© 1996 by Charles J. Alsheimer

All rights reserved. No portion of this publication may be reproduced or transmitted in any form or by any means, electronic or mechanical, including photocopy, recording, or any information storage and retrieval systems, without permission in writing from the publisher, except by a reviewer who may quote brief passages in a critical article or review to be printed in a magazine or newspaper, or electronically transmitted on radio or television.

Book design by Allen West, Krause Publications.

Published by

krause publications

700 E. State Street • Iola, WI 54990-0001

Please call or write for our free catalog of publications. Our toll-free number to place an order or to obtain a free catalog is (800) 258-0929. Please use our regular business telephone (715) 445-2214 for editorial comment and further information.

Library of Congress Catalog Number: 96-76703
ISBN: 0-87341-449-7

Printed in Canada

Dedication

Carla, I dedicate this book to you. You're the greatest.
In spite of a career of your own you are always there when I need you.
Thank you for being a wonderful wife and my best friend.

Contents

Foreword

I have had many blessings during my eighteen years of life, but perhaps the greatest of those blessings has been the relationship I've had with my father. Growing up as the son of Charlie Alsheimer has been an incredible experience.

I was two when dad left a good job in order to chase a dream. His dream was to become one of the world's top nature photographers, and it was a dream I ended up chasing with him as I tagged along through the outdoor world that became his new office.

His first few years in the photography business were undoubtedly tough. I often look back on his work from that time and wonder what inspired him to keep going. Evidently, it was the hope that he would one day make it to the top of his profession. That hope has become a reality. Years of hard work have led to the realization of his dream.

Although he has captured spectacular images of many species of wildlife, his portrayal of the white-tail deer is what has made him famous. His images of this amazing creature have appeared hundreds of times in books, magazines, calendars, posters, and catalogues. His style has become a favorite of all who have seen his work.

For several years now I have looked forward to the day when some of my dad's greatest photos would be contained within one book. Finally, this day has come. As you are about to see, the years of hard work have paid off in a big way. The essence of the whitetail can't be expressed better than it is in the following pages.

I have enjoyed witnessing this book come together during the past few months. Dad has put together a stunning portrayal of this truly stunning animal. I don't think I could be any more proud of him than I am at this moment. He has done a super job.

My dad's great love for the whitetail is evident throughout this book. Through the years, he has taught me to love this animal in the same way, and once you take a look at it as it is presented here, you too will fall in love with this great creature.

Aaron Alsheimer

Acknowledgments

The danger of doing an acknowledgments page is that no matter how hard you try, you wind up leaving someone out. This book has been a lifetime in the making, and along the way many wonderful people have been instrumental in making me who I am and played a part in whatever successes I've achieved. To all I'm deeply grateful. But along the way there have been some special people who truly took stock in me as a person and without knowing helped to make this book possible.

First, I'd like to thank my dad, Charles H. Alsheimer, for introducing me to the wonderful world of nature. Thanks, Pop.

Then I'd like to thank Haas Hargrave and Dick Snavely, two outstanding businessmen and outdoorsmen who encouraged me to pursue a career in the outdoor field when others said it was financially impossible. Their counsel birthed a dream that became a reality.

To Erwin "Joe" Bauer, Lenny Rue, and Mike Biggs. . . if there is such a thing as a hero in this business these super deer photographers fit the description. I've been fortunate to have photographed with all three. Thanks for keeping my fire lit.

I'm also indebted to Debbie Knauer, Pat Durkin, and the current *Deer and Deer Hunting* magazine team. The relationship I've forged with them over the years has been special.

To Paul Daniels, my neighbor, close friend, photography assistant, and in many ways the brother I never had, I say thanks for the memories.

To David Oathout, Bob and Alma Avery, thank you folks for loving me, making me a part of your family ten years ago and allowing me to photograph on your estate. Your mountain spread is the closest thing to heaven on earth.

My good friend and whitetail expert Ben Lingle, of Clearfield, Pennsylvania, has been an inspiration to me for years. He allowed me to photograph on his estate when no one knew who I was.

A special thanks is in order to my country neighbor and friend Craig Dougherty, one of the sharpest minds in the outdoor field. Thanks for all those fireside chats.

I offer a special thanks to Deborah Faupel and James Cihlar, my editors on this book. They are sharp people with great ideas and the energy to make things happen. Thanks for making this book a success.

To Jim and Charlie, thanks for giving me insight into the whitetail world not even the researchers know about. The time we've spent together in the wild has been one incredible blessing.

I offer a special thanks to my son Aaron for being there during the last eighteen years. From the Everglades to Alaska we've traveled in search of the next great photo. We didn't always get it but we gave it our best shot. Thanks for being my camera bearer, critic, model, hunting companion and most of all my buddy.

And most importantly I want to thank the Lord Jesus Christ for blessing me beyond measure. He's given me the greatest job on earth and without His guidance and direction this book never would have been possible.

Introduction

It has been said many times that the white-tailed deer is "America's deer." No other animal in North America captivates people as whitetails do. Nature lovers are in awe of their grace and beauty and hunters spend millions of dollars pursuing them each year. The phrase, "There's whitetails, then there's everything else when it comes to wildlife," is so true when it comes to North American wildlife.

Over the last twenty-five years I've been blessed to have photographed wildlife from the Everglades to Alaska. Through these experiences I've come to realize that no other animal can stack up to the whitetail when beauty, grace and compatibility with man are factored in. It is simply in a class by itself. This and more has caused me to devote more and more time to the whitetail with each passing year.

My infatuation with the whitetail began while growing up on a potato farm in Western New York State. Like so many farmers my dad was a deer hunter and he taught me the ways of the woods at an early age. Throughout the seasons I was able to view whitetails as they moved about the farm. They fascinated me whether they were bounding across a meadow or feeding in a hay field. In great part those early experiences fueled my desire to purchase camera equipment while serving with the United States Air Force in Vietnam during the late 1960s. When I returned home I took to our area's woods to try and capture the whitetail on film.

The beginning was not easy. In the early '70s there were few true wildlife photographers that I knew of, so everything I learned was by trial and error . . . mostly error. In spite of those early failures I pressed

on. Nature photography can be addicting and I was addicted. It was a hobby in the beginning but eventually became more than that. In 1979 I quit my sales and marketing position with a large corporation and devoted all my efforts to capturing nature on film. Though the bulk of my photography in the early '80s was whitetail related, I began branching out to photograph elk, moose, big horn sheep, and other western wildlife. I'd spent a lot of time with whitetails and wanted to know how they stacked up to the other animals in North America. Though I love the Rockies, Alaska, and the wildlife that lives there, I keep gravitating back to the whitetail. For the most part this is because I've never found any animal that intrigued me like *Odocoileus Virginianus.*

The last fifteen years have been a blessing beyond measure. During this time I've spent hundreds of hours sitting in deer blinds and sneaking through whitetail haunts trying to get "the right" photo. I learned long ago that good, tight portraits of whitetails are nice, but the thing that really tells the story about America's craftiest large animal is behavior. And behavior is what I love to photograph.

The key to much of the whitetail behavior I've been able to get over the years came to me by accident. While photographing on a large estate in the fall of 1986, I discovered a side of whitetails that has enabled me to truly get "up close and personal" with certain deer. One day while baiting around my photo blind I discovered a button buck staring at me from thirty yards away. Our eyes locked and I figured he'd run at any moment. When he didn't I tossed him some corn to see what he'd do. Well, to make a long story short I was able to get this buck and several other deer to "imprint" on the sound of shelled corn rattling around in a plastic can. The amazing thing is that by shaking the can I was able to get these deer to tolerate my presence. Interestingly that button buck lived to be nine years old. Over those nine years he allowed me to follow him in his wanderings, provided I had the food. In the end he wasn't a majestic looking buck, but he wore the scars of his nine years well. He had eluded predators, endured incredible buck fights, and survived the brutal northern winters before dying of what appeared to be natural causes. Rather than let coyotes consume his body I buried him beside a small stream, not unlike the small stream where we had met on a cool autumn day nine years before. Though it seems like a fairy tale, he and I formed a bond that's a true love story, one that will probably never be repeated in nature.

Since 1986 I have used the same imprinting technique on an estate in Pennsylvania, deer wintering areas in New York's Adirondack Mountains, a ranch in Texas, and here on our farm. Actually the principle is nothing new, Pavlov was the first to get a conditioned response from animals, and over the last ten years this technique has provided me a window into the whitetail's world few humans have ever seen. Lest you think I have some mysterious power over whitetails let me set the record straight: I've encountered many people from around the country who have also been able to get wild deer to imprint on foods and different sounds associated with it. So, what I've done is not new or unique, it's just that few people have discovered it.

After twenty-five years of intense photography I've been able to make some very interesting observations about whitetails. Early on I was amazed at how much they act like people when put in certain situations. Like humans, whitetails are extremely social, as you'll see in this book. As a result some deer are very outgoing while others keep to themselves. The latter are the toughest to observe and photograph. Some are very gentle and actually kind to other deer while others can be bullies, very mean, and down right aggressive. Fawns in particular remind me of toddlers. They want all kinds of affection from the doe and if they don't get it they do what amounts to whining and pouting in the deer world.

Does, on the other hand, probably impress me the most. They have the toughest job in insuring the species survives. They not only teach their fawns survival skills but also discipline and teach their offspring everything about the wild. They are incredible, and not unlike a loving human mother.

Though it is hard for some to understand, deer (because of their body and facial features) are as different from each other as we humans are. Photographers realize this more than anyone else, but most deer are easily recognized because of their looks and the way they walk.

The last fifteen years have been an incredible run, certainly an experience I never expected. During this time I've been fortunate to have been able to peer inside the whitetail world as few people have. As a result in the following pages you'll be able to get behind my camera's viewfinder with me and witness various aspects of the whitetail's world seldom seen. When you have turned the last page and looked at the last photo, I hope you'll have a greater appreciation for what I feel is the crown jewel of North American wildlife.

Charles J. Alsheimer
Bath, New York
February 28, 1996

About the Author

Born and raised on a farm in rural New York, Charles Alsheimer has devoted his life to photographing, writing, and lecturing on the beauty of God's creation. He is an award-winning nature photographer and outdoor writer, and one of the top white-tailed deer authorities in North America. During the course of the year he presents his multi-media nature programs to churches, civic clubs, organizations, and public schools across the country.

He is a field editor for *Deer and Deer Hunting* magazine. During the last twenty years Alsheimer's pursuit of the white-tailed deer and nature has taken him across North America. He has over one hundred national magazine cover photos to his credit and has written over two hundred published articles on the white-tailed deer. In addition his photos have won numerous state and national photo contests. He is the author of the popular book, *Whitetail: The Ultimate Challenge* and co-author of the book, *A Guide to Adirondack Deer Hunting.*

Alsheimer is an active member of the Outdoor Writers Association of America and the New York State Outdoor Writers Association. He has also served as a nature photography instructor for the National Wildlife Federation at their Nova Scotia, Blue Ridge, and Maine Summits.

A family man, he and his wife and son make their home near Bath in rural upstate New York, where they manage their 180 acre farm for wildlife.

Vital Statistics

I have so many fond memories of whitetails that it's difficult to say which one is the most lasting. After a lifetime of hunting, filming, and observing them, I'm in awe of their beauty, grace, and the incredible behavior they exhibit. Arguably, whitetails are the most majestic animal in the world. This is borne out by the millions of Americans who spend so much time hunting, photographing and watching them year-round. In addition to all this, the white-tailed deer has been able to adapt and thrive despite all that man has

thrown at it in the last 200 years. This is what has set it apart from other North American wildlife.

For centuries the American Indians were excellent stewards of what God had entrusted to them. When the first settlers arrived on the shores of North America, they found a land teeming with an array of wildlife. The early settlers encountered everything from songbirds to bears, but quickly realized that the white-tailed deer was the most important species. The whitetail's pre-colonial numbers are not known for sure, but best accounts

put North America's whitetail population at over twenty million when the Pilgrims arrived at Plymouth Rock. Unfortunately, it didn't take long for this to change.

After the Civil War, America changed dramatically. For one thing there was a great westward movement of people. Also, much of the eastern portion of the United States' forests was cleared for farming and industry, destroying millions of acres of wildlife habitat in the process. During this time there were open seasons and no bag limits on

In the northern portion of their range, white-tailed fawns are born in late May and early June. Weighing in at around six pounds, these little beauties grow rapidly and by summer's end can fend for themselves.

The size difference between a mature white-tailed buck and a fawn is substantial. This photo, taken in early September, is an oddity because of the fawn's condition. This fawn was probably born in late July or early August and will have a difficult time surviving the upcoming winter.

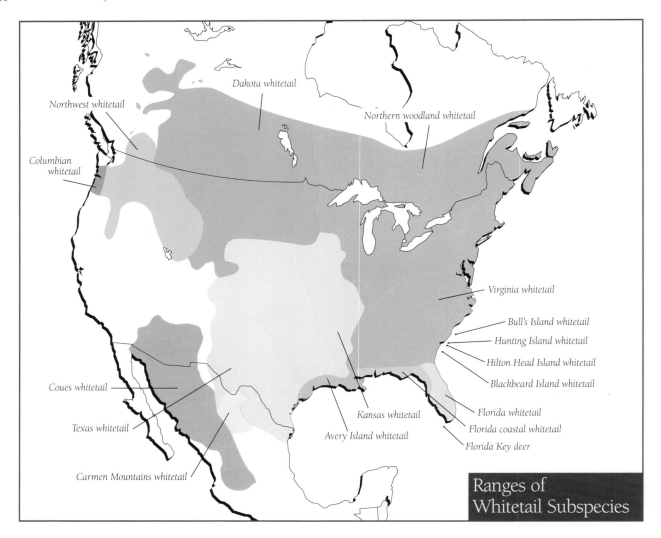

Northwest whitetail

Dakota whitetail

Northern woodland whitetail

Columbian whitetail

Virginia whitetail

Bull's Island whitetail

Hunting Island whitetail

Hilton Head Island whitetail

Blackbeard Island whitetail

Coues whitetail

Texas whitetail

Kansas whitetail

Avery Island whitetail

Florida whitetail

Florida coastal whitetail

Florida Key deer

Carmen Mountains whitetail

Ranges of Whitetail Subspecies

whitetails and other wildlife. The market hunting of wildlife, particularly the whitetail, became popular in order to fill the meat demands of the eastern cities. With nature being unable to meet man's needs, this "progress" caused a drastic plunge in all wildlife populations by the late 1800s. It is estimated that on the eve of 1900 America's whitetail population was about 500,000, just a fraction of what it once was.

Fortunately, America's sportsmen reacted to this decline in the nick of time. At their urging, open seasons on whitetails were closed and nearly all wildlife was protected from market hunting. The recovery was slow and it took decades for whitetail numbers to increase in the eastern portion of the United States. The whitetail's proliferation rate is legendary,

and by the 1950s the whitetail population was firmly restored to its original numbers. It wasn't long before the whitetail expanded its range by moving into America's west, and north into the western Canadian provinces that bordered the United States.

Today it is estimated that there are more whitetails in North America than at any other time in history. It is the most plentiful antlered animal on the continent, with thirty recognized subspecies. These subspecies range from as far north as the 52nd parallel in Canada to the equator in the south, and their size varies greatly over their range. In the northern reaches of the whitetail's range, a mature buck will be about forty-two inches tall at the shoulder, while in the southernmost region, a buck will be little more than half as tall. In many por-

The Northern Woodland subspecies is the largest and most beautiful of all whitetails and is admired by millions across its range.

In spite of a small body size as compared to their northern cousins, the Texas subspecies living in the brush country of south Texas sports antlers as large as those of any whitetails living elsewhere on the continent.

tions of North America it is common for whitetail bucks to weigh over three hundred pounds. The largest known whitetail was harvested by archer John Annett of Ontario, Canada, in 1977. It dressed out at 431 pounds on government-certified scales and is estimated to have had a live weight of over five hundred pounds.

Though the whitetail is far from the largest animal in North America, it is unquestionably the most graceful of all antlered animals. Simply put, a whitetail is poetry in motion. Its ability to run up to forty miles per hour, leap thirty feet with a single bound, change direction on a dime, and when pushed leap over an eight-foot-high fence says volumes about its athletic ability. As awesome as these physical attributes are, there is more to say about this unique animal. Collectively its senses are more

finely tuned than any large animal roaming the continent. This is the prime reason it has been able to survive in man's backyard when other wildlife has not. In other portions of this book I'll describe experiences where I've seen firsthand just how good a whitetail's sense of smell, eyesight, and hearing are. However, I'll preface these examples by saying these three far exceed that of humans. The fact that a whitetail has over ten times greater nasal surface area than a human says much about its ability to smell danger long before man even realizes there is a problem.

Just because whitetails do not have the ability to reason as humans do, don't think for a minute they are dumb creatures. More than once I've been witness to their intelligence, and it can make even the smartest person sit up and take notice. Dennis

A whitetail's athletic ability is legendary. It's not uncommon for one to be able to jump thirty feet with a single bound. Clearing a fifteen-foot stream is a simple task for a whitetail. This buck was standing still when it decided to cross to the other side.

How high can a whitetail jump? Conditions dictate the answer. Keen whitetail observers have seen bucks clear eight-foot-high fences. This buck was chasing a doe and opted to jump the cattle fence rather than going under it.

White-tailed bucks know exactly how much room they need to get their antlers through a tight space. Because of this they will often go under a fence rather than jumping it. Does will almost always go under a fence if they have a choice.

Olson, author of *Way of the Whitetail,* writes a very fitting description of just how smart a whitetail is. "Of course, we value intellect as the trait of 'higher' animals. Deer are long on instinct and short on our version of logic. They are rather stupid, compared to us and our computer, satellites and complicated business deals. But, if just once we could let deer design an IQ test, the first question might be, Which odors on the wind right now are edible, which are dangerous, and which are neutral? Who flunks that test?" Olson's quote says much about the whitetail's intelligence and constantly reminds me of why whitetails so often outsmart me.

Time and time again I've observed their ability to remember things in their environment. One of the best examples I can think of is their ability to know the time of day. For several years I've been feeding the deer on our farm with an electronic feeder during the summer months. To get the best photo opportunities I set the feeder's timer to go off at 7 a.m. and 6 p.m. Regardless of the amount of daylight, several members of a doe group show up and stand around looking at the feeder. . . exactly five minutes before the feeder goes off. It's incredible. Try getting a human to be on time like this, with or without a watch!

Whitetails are the ultimate survival machine. If given a choice they will spend much of their time in thick cover, venturing out only in darkness. This behavior makes them very hard to find.

Whitetails are famous for their food consumption. During the course of a year each deer will eat, on average, over one ton of food. In farm country and urban areas, where numbers are high, this can cause significant crop and habitat damage.

Whitetails know their territory like we know the streets in our neighborhood. And the least little disturbance in their turf. . . the hanging of a tree stand or the placement of a photo blind. . . puts them on red alert. Without exaggeration they know every natural object in their home environment. They are nature's ultimate survival machine, and by the time whitetail bucks or does reach three-and-a-half years of age, they are nearly impossible to fool.

A whitetail's life is a journey of trials, tribulations, and triumphs woven into the seasons of their lives. They are truly amazing animals. In the next few chapters I'll share with you their personality, grace, and beauty blended through seldom-seen behavior.

Whitetails and turkeys share the same range—where you find one you will find the other. In some regions they compete heavily for mast in the fall of the year.

A whitetail's ability to flee from danger is incredible. They are capable of running up to forty miles per hour, and their combined sense of smell, hearing and eyesight is unsurpassed.

Once autumn arrives, white-tailed bucks begin rubbing their antlers on trees in preparation for the upcoming rut.

CHAPTER 2

Blossom Time

No doubt most people view spring in a whitetail's life as a time of wildflowers and pretty, spotted fawns. Actually, in the northern portion of its range such sights do not occur until late May, at the tail end of springtime. Before fawns and wildflowers show up, many things take place during a whitetail's spring.

Determining seasonal splits in a whitetail's life can be difficult. In nature there are no hard and fast rules when it comes to determining seasons. Rather, moving from one season to another is a gradual process, especially in the north. Of all the whitetail seasons, spring always seems to be the slowest in coming. Unlike the other seasonal changes, winter is usually reluctant to give up her reign. The tug-of-war between winter and spring seems to unfold each year as snow and sleet battle spotty days of warm sunshine. It can be quite a show in the northern part of North America.

Those who study nature consider March's solar equinox the pivotal point in separating winter and spring. By the time March 21st rolls around, the longer days, often with warm rays of sunshine, begin to break up the ice and snow in the north. For the first time in nearly four months the ground begins to warm and comes back to life, causing what is known as spring green-up. At this time, after spending months on their winter range, whitetails begin moving back to their familiar summer territory. For farmland whitetails this movement may mean only a two to four-mile shift. For deer inhabiting northern forest regions a movement of up to twenty miles or more is not uncommon once the signs of spring arrive.

When spring green-up finally arrives whitetails are not very pretty sights. As the days get longer their winter hair sheds and their summer coat begins growing in.

Food can be scarce in early spring, causing all whitetails to fight with each other for available supplies. When such bouts are between a doe and her fawn it vividly illustrates how unforgiving nature can be when it comes to survival.

By the time winter breaks a white-tailed deer is gaunt looking. Fortunately this appearance is only temporary. Through a process known as photoperiodism the increase in daylight causes them to begin shedding their winter coat. Where deer densities are great it's not uncommon to see the ground specked here and there with the shed hair. Frequently I've watched deer pull loose hair from their bodies by shaking, biting, and scratching themselves with their hooves. Whitetails are extremely social and it's quite common to see them grooming each other during this time, removing their partners' hair in the process.

The increase in daylight triggers a need for greater food intake, and both bucks and does gravitate to whatever greenery they can find. In the early part of spring, finding green shoots of grasses can be difficult. As a result, aggressive behavior often occurs as bucks, does and fawns compete with each other for available food. The cruelty of nature is evident when a doe fights off her fawns for food. In the natural world it's everyone for themselves when the going gets tough; and though I photograph this behavior each spring, it's not something I can get used to.

In the northern region white-tailed bucks begin growing their antlers in early April. As the antlers grow, they are encased in a network of blood vessels and skin tissue called velvet, which nourishes the antlers throughout the growth process. At first the growing process is slow, with only an inch or two of growth occurring by the end of April. But with the arrival of May the growing process kicks into high gear. With more and more daylight each day, antler growth accelerates dramatically, with the peak

growth occurring from mid-June to late July, when the days are longest. Though no two bucks grow their antlers at the same rate the growing process is normally complete by August 10th. After this the velvet-coated antlers begin to dry down and harden. Then, around the end of August bucks begin peeling their velvet.

Bucks move very little and become almost secretive once their antlers begin growing. During this time their hormonal level is at the lowest point of the year so they are not very aggressive. They spend spring and summer with other bucks. By being easy-going and avoiding conflict their velvet-covered antlers are seldom damaged.

One of nature's signals that fawning time is close at hand is when leaves begin to bud out in the north. During this time a whitetail doe has much to

This is a scene I never get used to seeing. As a white-tailed doe nears her fawning time she deliberately drives off her fawn from the previous year. Though not pleasant to observe, it insures that her fawns will take up residence elsewhere and eliminate any chance of inbreeding when they become adults.

In spite of being in the early stages of antler growth, this buck feverishly works a scrape's overhanging licking branch. Though this is seldom seen outside of the autumn months, bucks have a strong desire to work scrapes year-round. Over the years I've been able to photograph such behavior many times.

deal with. For one thing she's heavy with fawns. For another she must deal with the harsh task of driving off her fawns from the year before. This is essential for a healthy deer herd. By physically forcing her buck fawn to leave her and the area, she is insuring that interbreeding will not take place when the male fawn reaches breedable age.

The true beauty of spring is the rebirth of nature, both flora and fauna. I love all seasons, but spring and autumn are my favorites. Few things in nature can top the fresh smell of the forest as the last snows vanish, hearing the first peepers, seeing the gradual budding of leaves, or witnessing the birth of a fawn. These are just a few of the things

When spring green-up is complete and vegetation is lush, bucks (and insects) begin to show themselves at the fringes of day as they forage in the fields. By late May their antlers' growth becomes quite visible.

that make springtime so special and the latter is enough to melt the heart of any nature lover.

The whitetail's fawning season is kind of like frosting on spring's cake. After a gestation period of two hundred days the bulk of whitetail fawns are born in late May or early June in the north. Because they are born during the season's warm days and nights, fawns are able to miss the unpredictable weather of early spring and have a better chance of survival.

If conditions are right does will give birth to two fawns. Generally one will be a buck and one a doe and they'll weigh from six to nine pounds, with their bodies being about the size of a loaf of bread. To say they are very vulnerable at this stage is an understatement. Their survival is dependant

on the doe, with many factors going into whether the newborns make it through the first week of their life.

It's critical that the fawns are born in habitat that allows them to hide from patrolling predators. Once born, the doe ingests all afterbirth, cleans the birth area, and bathes the newborn fawns to keep predators from locating them. Usually a fawn will be able to walk within a half hour of birth and be able to walk up to several hundred yards within the first hour. In order to stay one step ahead of prey animals the doe will move the fawns shortly after birth and constantly move them to different bedding sites during the first few weeks after birth. Also, to increase survivability a doe will force twin fawns to bed apart and feed them only two or three times a day. Seldom does the doe bed with the newborns, choosing to stay just out of range in case predators should come by. If this happens she will spring into action and come to the fawn's rescue.

Though the doe attempts to have the fawns bed apart, it can sometimes turn into quite a chore to make sure that it happens. Fawns imprint easily and are extremely social, therefore they have a tendency to want to be with their mother or their sibling. Years ago I came to the realization that a whitetail's behavior is similar to human behavior. Fawns, like small children, are often strong-willed and don't always want to do what they are instructed to do. On several occasions I've photographed does attempting to bed fawns apart, only to have them try to get closer to each other when the doe leaves. It can be rather humorous to watch, especially when the doe uses her own form of discipline to get the obedience she is looking for.

The accompanying photo shows two fawns that I photographed bedded together. Though I photographed them at close range I was careful not to disturb them or the area. To insure my own safety I continually scanned the woods for the doe. The photo illustrates how vulnerable they are. They never made any attempt to move or flee from me. This vividly shows how easy they would be to kill should a wolf, coyote, or fox come upon them. Because of this I seldom pursue newborn fawns to photograph. It's just not worth it to the animal. Rather, I wait until they have fully imprinted on the doe and are able to run from danger.

After a gestation period of two hundred days, the bulk of white-tailed fawns are born in late May and early June in the north. Immediately after the birth the doe thoroughly cleans her newborn to free it of any odors that will attract predators.

Weighing six to nine pounds at birth, fawns quickly respond to the doe's commands. A newborn will be able to walk within an hour of birth and is able to walk several hundred yards after the first hour.

Witnessing the way a doe communicates with her fawns is a special experience. When a doe seeks out a fawn at feeding time she will approach the fawn's bedding area giving off mews and low grunts. Upon hearing the doe's call, the fawn will rise from its bed and often prance to the doe's side before locking on to her nipples and ingesting up to eight ounces of nourishing milk. The feeding takes less than a minute. Throughout the nursing process the fawn's tail wags excitedly while the doe grooms the frisky fawn or fawns. Once the nursing is complete, the doe continues to groom the fawn before walking off with her family in tow.

In order to instill Nature's harshness upon their fawns, a doe will not pamper her offspring. Oh, you can be sure she'll shower them with all kinds of love and affection. But she is a strong discipli-

If conditions are right, does will give birth to two fawns. Their survival is dependant on the doe, with many factors going into whether the newborns make it through the first week of their life.

This photo shows just how easy it is for a white-tailed fawn to imprint on another animal if its mother is killed. Muffin, the canine pet of wildlife rehabilitator Cynthia Palmer of Avoca, N.Y., was nursing six of her own offspring when two baby raccoons and an orphaned fawn were turned over to her in early June of 1981. The dog accepted the orphans and nursed them for a month and a half. Cynthia released the fawn and coons back into the wild after they were weaned.

narian as well. She picks the bedding sites, she decides when to feed them and what to let them be subjected to, and when they do not obey her, she is quick to physically discipline them. If a fox or coyote gets too close to a fawn during the first few weeks after birth, the doe will either charge the predator or attempt to get it to follow her to lead them away from the fawn's bedding location. Also, should a doe hear her fawn bleating, she'll come on a run to rescue it. I've witnessed how well a doe can use her front hoofs, and it's nothing I'd want to mess with.

Seldom have I seen a doe let a buck or another doe get close to her fawn during the first month of life. On those occasions when I've seen a curious buck approach a fawn, the doe was quick to let him know she was in charge. One of the amazing things I discovered early in my photography career was that most bucks shied away from mature does because of the does' aggressiveness. Does have a tendency to rule the woods when fawns are vulnerable.

By the time the summer equinox arrives most fawns are large enough to outrun most of their enemies and begin bedding and traveling with the doe wherever she goes. Though the fawns still nurse, they are beginning to fend for themselves and are ready to face the next phase of their life.

By late spring the buck's antlers are nearing their halfway point of development. Bucks are very secretive now and spend time bedding, feeding and grooming with other bachelor bucks. Seldom will bucks and does be seen together during this time.

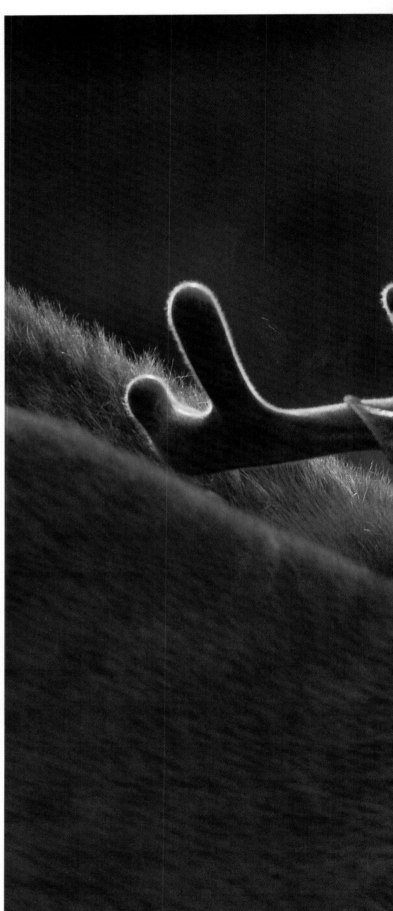

CHAPTER 3

The Longest Season

The early morning fog was as thick as honey as I stepped from the road into the dew laden grass. In spite of near darkness I was able to negotiate my twelve-pound camera and tripod through the swale grass and tag alders. My goal was to make it to my photo blind along the edge of a shallow pond before the last whitetail bedded for the day. It didn't take me long to cover the three-hundred yards and ready myself for the morning's offering. Dawn comes quickly in July and the rising sun began turning the sky's ribbons of clouds into a red and purple rainbow. With the light increasing by the minute I could see the thermals moving the fog's backlit beads of water back and forth. The sight was almost hypnotic. On the far side of the pond I could barely make out a muskrat swimming along the pond's shore. As I sat there gripping my camera I took in the blessing unfolding before me. The experience was so invigorating that I almost forgot why I was there.

To my right the morning's stillness was broken with the swishing sound of grass moving. Twenty yards from me a doe and two fawns moved to the water's edge. Slowly the doe and fawns ventured into the shallow pond and began drinking. Though only a little over a month old, the spotted fawns seemed quite large. First one fawn then the other dipped his head under the doe's belly and began nursing. For a second I thought their tugging was going to tear their mother apart. The fawns' jostling didn't seem to phase the doe and for the half minute they nursed she maternally stood still and groomed them. With breakfast complete, the threesome poked their way further into the pond, and when all three reached the center the fawns began splashing around, resembling two small kids having a water fight. Unfortunately, I didn't have enough light to photo-

graph, so I just sat back and observed. With water flying in every direction, the doe watched as her fawns raced back and forth across the pond in a helter skelter fashion. After nearly five minutes the fawns calmed down and the three disappeared into the high grass at the far side of the pond.

Within minutes, with enough photography light now present, the doe returned to the pond and walked from one end to the other, with the two fawns in tow, before disappearing into the tag alders. During their water march I shot several frames to help remind me of the magnificent show they provided. Nothing else showed up the rest of the morning, but the half hour spectacular said much about the beauty and grace of whitetails.

Compared with other times of the year, summer is relatively uneventful for whitetails. During this time does are busy nursing and caring for their young in preparation for the upcoming winter months. In June and July fawns grow by leaps and bounds and command center stage for those who love nature. Their beauty, innocence, and playful behavior make them a precious commodity.

When summer arrives whitetails become extremely secretive. By late June a doe's fawns are big enough, and fast enough, to travel with her night and day. Usually the doe's female offspring from the year before joins her mother and fawns to form a family group, which will stay together until the yearling doe has her first fawns the following spring, when she is two years old. On occasion I've seen two or three adult does traveling together with their fawns, but my experience has shown this to be rare, at least during the summer.

It's during the summer months that I begin to step up my photographic pursuit of fawns. If they have never experienced humans they are fairly easy

Bucks occasionally fight during the summer, but not with their antlers. Rather, they stand on their hind legs and flail with their hooves. This dominance behavior often sorts out who is boss by summer's end.

to call within camera range. Often I'll go to a known feeding or bedding area and use a combination of fawn bleats (a high-pitched *kneeee!*) and doe grunts to bring them within camera range. There are few animals in nature more curious than a white-tailed fawn, and they often come looking for what's making the fawn bleat. Over the years this has resulted in many photo opportunities.

The reason for my seldom calling fawns during the latter part of spring is my fear of having them come to the call and possibly imprint on me. Once while photographing does along a stream I used a

fawn bleat call and wound up having a fawn come right up to me. The little "skipper" proceeded to follow me, and it took quite a bit of effort to convince it that it shouldn't hang around humans. Fawns are too impressionable the first couple weeks of their life, and it's critical that they bond to their mothers in order to gain vital survival skills.

"Summertime and the living is easy," are the words to a once popular song. This aptly describes the whitetail's life during this period. Except in the most remote portions of their range, whitetails are grazers during the summer months, relying heavily on wild strawberries, alfalfa, clover and other grasses. During hot days and warm nights, bucks, does, and fawns spend most of their time bedded.

In 1991 the New York State Department of Environmental Conservation (NYSDEC) began radio collaring western New York whitetails to study the timing of movements to and from winter range. In all, they wound up collaring twenty-two bucks and does. Though the study has dealt with winter movements, the deer are monitored throughout the year. Our farm is part of the study area, and it has been fascinating to see just how little these deer move, especially during summer. In one case a particular doe was located in the same small brush lot day after day during the fawning season. She probably ventured out and about during the cover of darkness but returned to the same place by daylight. The bottom line is: as long as cover, food and water are present, whitetails are content to stay in one place during the summer months.

By the end of August white-tailed fawns have taken their mother to her limit. The long days of feeding and nurturing have given the doe a low tolerance level when it comes to her relationship with her offspring. Even though the fawns are capable of being weaned by eight weeks of age, they still want a daily dose of nursing, which isn't always what the doe has in mind. Often I've seen a doe's short fuse and rejection of a fawn's desire to nurse by summer's end. Many times I've intently watched does and fawns from my photo blind during this time and the doe's body language appeared to be saying, "will you guys leave me alone. . . stop bugging me. . . please! . . . go chase a butterfly."

Bucks on the other hand spend their summers

During the summer months bucks are creatures of the edge and move only at the fringes of daylight.

By late summer the majority of white-tailed fawns are weaned and become more and more independent with each passing day.

differently. For one thing they have only themselves to worry about. With a lot of idle time they bed during the day and feed mostly at night. They also become quite social and form bachelor groups. Two types of bachelor groups often exist within a buck population. The first is made up of yearling bucks. As mentioned in the previous chapter, when a yearling buck is run off by the doe, just prior to her giving birth, the year-old buck wanders to new territory. During the process, it meets up with other yearling bucks. Because mature bucks often reject yearlings these young bucks usually wind up gravitating to each other. As a result, in areas with good whitetail populations, it's not uncommon to see upwards of five or more yearling bucks together throughout the summer. Mature bucks, on the other hand, tend to form mature bachelor groups or keep to themselves. On occasion mature bucks will accept one or two yearling bucks to their group, and it's the mature buck's personality that often dictates whether or not this will happen. Regardless, bucks seldom mingle with does during the summer. About the only time you'll see them close to each other is when they feed in a hay field or other common food source.

Though the scientific literature doesn't mention it, often white-tailed bucks exhibit some rutting behavior during the spring and summer months, when their antlers are covered with velvet. On many occasions I've seen and photographed white-tailed bucks working a scrape's licking branch while the bucks were in various stages of antler growth. In most of the cases I've observed, however, they did not paw the ground free of debris as they do in the autumn months. Also, bucks begin lip-curling or Flehmening with increased frequency by August. This is no doubt brought on by an increase in the level of the sex hormone testosterone in the buck's body. Flehmening takes place when a buck smells a doe's urine in an attempt to see if she is ready to breed.

With June's long daily photoperiod, a buck's antlers grow rapidly. As mentioned in Chapter 2, these growing masses of bone are very sensitive, and because of this bucks curtail much of their activity during June and July. In August, as the days begin to get shorter, photoperiodism slows antler growth and the antler bone begins to harden. Also at about this time photoperiodism triggers the growth of a whitetail's winter coat and the increase of the male sex hormone, testosterone. During the process a deer's fur appears to be blotchy as the brown thicker hair replaces the thin reddish summer hair.

As August winds down the nights become cooler and cooler, especially in the north. By the end of August a buck's velvet-covered antlers have hardened. As the velvet dries it begins to crack, and in some cases the points of a buck's antlers prick through the velvet covering, setting the stage for the peeling process. In the north I've witnessed and photographed bucks peeling velvet from August 25th to September 20th, with the bulk of it happening during the five days either side of September 1st.

I've always been fascinated by the whitetail's annual antler cycle, from the time the bucks start to grow them in the spring until they cast them in winter. As a hunter and photographer, I've observed and photographed all stages of this cycle many times during the past fifteen years. One aspect of the antler process, the peeling of velvet, is something few have observed.

With velvet-covered antlers nearly full grown, a white-tailed buck works a scrape's overhanging licking branch. This behavior will be sporadic until the velvet is peeled. When October bursts onto the scene, full blown scraping will begin.

By late summer, with antlers fully grown, whitetails in bachelor groups become more active and can be seen at the fringes of day wherever they are found.

Buck fawns begin exhibiting their male behavior even before their spots disappear. It's not uncommon to see them try to mount their fawn sister or their mother.

With testosterone levels on the increase, bucks begin showing some rutting behavior before their velvet is peeled. This buck has just smelled where a doe has urinated and is Flehmening in an attempt to tell if she is in estrus. This behavior will become more and more prevalent as the calendar inches toward November and the breeding season.

One sign that autumn is close at hand is a whitetail losing its summer coat. This is a result of photoperiodism; by September a northern whitetail's winter fur will have replaced its red summer-coat of hair.

In August of 1989 I photographed this buck peeling his velvet from start to finish. It took him only fifty minutes to complete the process. During this time he went from flurry to near exhaustion as he tried to free the bloody velvet from his antlers.

When the last strand of velvet was free, the buck sniffed the ground, picked the velvet up in his mouth, and ate it. Seldom have I seen so much energy expended by a whitetail in so short a period of time.

Few white-tailed bucks grow antlers this large. For the better part of four hours I watched as he tried to get the last strands of velvet off his bloody antlers.

On August 31, 1989, while photographing on a large preserve, I was able to record this phenomenon on film. When I first located the buck at 7:00 a.m. in a swampy area, a small piece of velvet had already started peeling from one of the antler tines. From the time I started photographing, it took the buck fifty minutes to completely strip the velvet from his antlers.

During the fifty-minute period, I was amazed at the buck's behavior in attempting to strip his antlers clean. Throughout the process, he periodically licked all the blood off the alder bush he was rubbing before he peeled more of the velvet from his antlers. As more and more velvet began hanging from the antlers, the buck became violent in his attempts to remove the velvet. Several times the buck stopped, panted, and once staggered backwards, appearing to be exhausted. On two occasions he actually stopped and rested before continuing. After he freed all the velvet from his antlers, the buck scented the ground to locate the pieces that had been peeled off. Then, to my surprise, the buck picked up the velvet and ate it. I have since learned that bucks commonly eat their velvet, perhaps a behavioral trait to prevent predators from locating them.

One thing that sticks in my mind is the speed at which the buck removed the velvet and the violence involved in the velvet shedding process. I've photographed several buck fights over the years, and none was as violent as this buck's behavior. The annoyance of blood dripping and velvet hanging in its eyes probably contributed to this behavior.

For all practical purposes the velvet-peeling process and the winter-coat growing signal an end to the whitetail's summer. This sets the stage for what I view as the whitetail's grandest season. . . autumn, with all its splendor.

Most healthy does give birth to twins. On rare occasions some does have triplets.

Autumn's Splendor

Whitetails have a real sweet tooth. When apples begin falling from the trees they gorge themselves until all the available fruit is gone.

As the earth turns on its axis, each day becomes increasingly shorter, setting the stage for nature's seasonal crown jewel. Autumn is my favorite season for so many reasons. The cool frosty mornings, the freshness of the air, hillsides painted with a rainbow of reds and golds and the splendor of wildlife-filled woods makes me feel younger, more vibrant and thankful for all God has done for me. When I think of autumn my pulse quickens and my senses get a little keener. For me autumn is nature's Christmas present delivered three months early. And the white-tailed deer has much to do with why I feel this way.

By the time late September and early October arrive, the nights are cool and the year's crop of apples and mast start falling from the trees.

Conditions are at their peak, and it's the grandest time of the year for whitetails. It's also the time when the greatest changes take place in a whitetail's life. As September eases into October, the whitetail's thick winter coat grows in. This heavier coat, coupled with autumn's warm days, causes whitetails to be less active during daylight hours. During this time bucks usually stay separate from does and seldom venture out of their core area. On the other hand, does are biologically different and seem to continue their normal movement patterns. As a result, doe sightings are often much higher than buck sightings in September and October.

During the early autumn months food dictates deer movement. Whitetail bucks commonly lose up to 25% of their body weight by the end of the

During the fall when their estrogen level begins to increase, does become more active and it's not uncommon for them to fight with other does in their family group.

When October's frosty mornings arrive, bucks begin to work scrapes in a more predictable fashion. They rub their preorbital, nasal, and forehead glands and they salivate on the scrape's overhanging licking branch to leave as much scent as possible at the scrape site. This lets other deer know of their presence.

As bucks' testosterone levels increase they begin to spar with one another. These matches are merely shoving matches and preludes to the vicious fights they may get into when the full-blown breeding begins. Unlike true fights, which are often brief, sparring matches can last a half hour or more.

breeding season so they spend September and October building fat reserves. Because of the white-tail's innate ability to determine which food is the most nutritious they gravitate to apple orchards, hay and corn fields, and mast producing forests in the north.

When September arrives bucks begin reacting to the increased testosterone in their system. This natural sex drug causes them to rub their antlers and spar with the other bucks in their bachelor group. They also begin to work scrapes as well as lip curl whenever they come upon a spot where a doe has urinated.

Though the whitetail's peak breeding time varies throughout the United States the activity associated with it is the same whether it's viewed in Texas, New York, or Canada. When mid-October arrives in the North the rutting switch is thrown inside a buck's body. The days are shorter, cooler, and a few of the older class does come into estrus (the time when does are able to be bred) by mid-October. All this triggers the chase, rub, and scrape phase of the rut. Also, the closer the buck to doe ratio is to 1 to 1 the more dense the rutting sign will be. The rutting frenzy will intensify for approximately thirty days and climax when the majority of the does come into estrus, which in most northern regions occurs in November.

By mid-October in the north, a buck's bachelor group begins to break up. When this happens it's not uncommon for a buck's range to increase from 600 - 4,000 acres during the rut, when they are constantly on the move searching for receptive does.

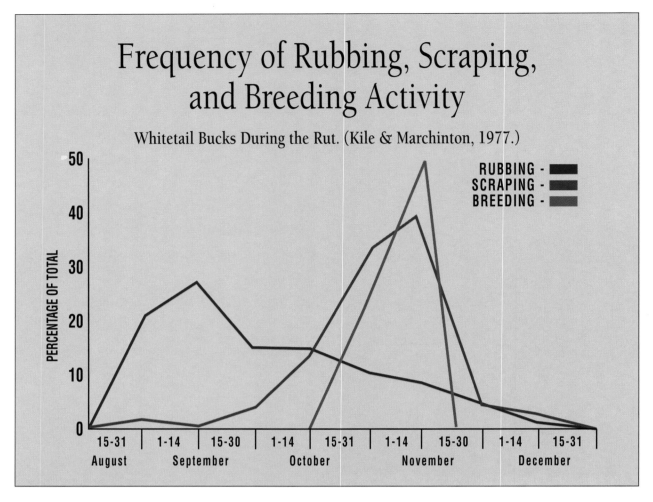

Frequency of Rubbing, Scraping, and Breeding Activity

Whitetail Bucks During the Rut. (Kile & Marchinton, 1977.)

RUBBING -
SCRAPING -
BREEDING -

The Chase Phase

Once September has passed, things begin changing rapidly for a whitetail buck. With October's arrival comes a greater infusion of testosterone. This not only causes a buck's attitude to change but it also causes them to cover more ground. During the rut it's common for a buck's range to encompass anywhere from 600 to 3,000 acres or more as it searches for receptive does.

Around the end of October bucks are literally making a scrape wherever an adequate licking branch presents itself. They work the branch above the ground. Once they have left their scent on the branch they then paw the ground out under the branch. This may seem hard to believe, but through the years I've observed over 500 bucks at scrapes and the tendency is for bucks to work near-

ly every overhanging branch they encounter. Because the majority of these scrapes are a result of an instinctive action brought on by a buck's sex drive, most will not be revisited. However, some of these scrapes, because of their location, will become prime scrapes for bucks when November and the peak of the rut arrives. In a sense the primary scrapes become almost like whitetail "bus stations" with several bucks using the same scrape.

Throughout whitetail country November bursts onto the scene. Now the mornings are frosty and in some cases snow flurries fill the air. Bucks are on the move. Around the first week of November it seems as though all bucks get yet another infusion of testosterone. With their latest fix, scraping, rubbing and aggression are at their highest. The entire deer family quickly realizes that

When acorn mast begins falling from the trees, all whitetails gravitate to this very nutritional food source. In years when there is an abundance of acorns, deer can be easily observed in such locations throughout the fall and winter months.

By the time late October arrives, a whitetail's thick winter coat has grown in. During periods of rain they must constantly shake to rid themselves of the water that's soaked into their coat.

By the time the leaves have fallen from the trees, bucks begin actively pursuing all does in their area in an attempt to find one that is ready to breed. By trapping the scent from a doe's urine in their nose, and Flehmening, a buck can tell which doe is in or coming into estrus.

In spite of a doe's fawns being weaned in August, she still occasionally allows them to nurse throughout the fall.

a mature buck is nothing to mess with. A buck with several ruts under his belt not only chases every doe he encounters but he also wants to kill the bachelor bucks he spent the summer with. The woods seem chaotic for most of the deer, especially the does and fawns.

During this time the doe family groups try to steer clear of any buck. Does know full well the lethality of a buck's antlers and try to avoid any contact with them. As a result a doe that is not ready to stand for a buck and be bred flees for her life. This is how the "Chase Phase" portion of the whitetail rut gets its name. With the does in hiding bucks are on the move night and day trying to locate one that is in estrus.

With the arrival of November, breeding begins in the northern portions of the whitetail's range. If two

mature bucks find themselves vying for the same doe, a fight to the death may ensue. If it does, the fight's sound is incredible as antler bashing, grunting, moaning, and brush breaking fill the woods for hundreds of yards all around. The sound attracts any buck who wants a piece of the breeding action. Once the breeding becomes full-blown, buck sightings decrease. With estrous smell in the air, nearly every hot doe has a buck in her thicket. Because an estrous doe smells right for up to seventy-two hours, a buck will stay with her and possibly breed her several times during this period. With the does now in charge, the only buck movement to be found is when a doe decides to move about to feed or a buck has completed his job of procreation and moves on to the next encounter. Chapter 5 vividly shows the Chase Phase and how it unfolds, from the chase, to fighting, to the breeding.

As November winds down, fewer does are in heat and bucks begin to move again, looking for receptive does. November's thirty days have taken a heavy toll on a buck's body. The scars of fighting can be death warrants and in some cases, as stated earlier, bucks lose between 25 and 30 percent of their body weight. The weight loss alone causes many bucks to teeter on the edge of survival, as they face the prospects of winter.

Rubbing

As the rut inches closer to its November peak, white-tailed bucks increase their rubbing activity to both strengthen neck muscles and also to let other bucks know they are present. In the process of making rubs, whereby they rub their antlers on tree trunks, bucks leave their visual calling card. In addition to being dominant markers, rubs are also scent posts. When rubbing their antlers on the tree trunk, bucks rub their forehead gland and nose on the rub, and will almost always lick the rub surface to leave their distinct odor. Though other bucks can visually relate the size of the rub to the size of the animal, it's the odor left on the rub by a buck's forehead gland that often lets other bucks know who's been there. It's been my experience that this, as much as the size of the rub, determines an adult buck's social status within a given territory. Also researchers believe that the scent (pheromones) bucks leave on rubs serves as a priming function that influences the timing of the rut.

After witnessing hundreds of "battles" between bucks and tree trunks I've concluded that there are basically three kinds of rubbing behavior: random, traditional, and aggressive. Random rubbing is a byproduct of increased testosterone in a buck's system and his desire to leave his calling card. He does this by randomly rubbing trees while roaming his territory. At times there appears to be a pattern to these rubs (i.e., along travel corridors) but more often random rubs will appear wherever a buck feels the urge to rub.

Traditional rubs occur more often in a balanced deer herd where there are many mature bucks with the rub being rubbed year after year. Such rubs are usually found on larger trees with generations of whitetails leaving their mark and scent for other deer to see.

Aggressive rubs are a result of a buck's attitude at a given time and are caused by competition within the buck population. During the fall of 1991 I was able to keep close tabs on several mature bucks who were vying for dominance. This, coupled with a very good buck to doe ratio, made for some interesting moments on the Adirondack property where I was photographing. One morning in late October I observed a large eight pointer as it followed a doe from the feeding area. It was obvious that the doe was nearing estrus. During the previous hour the big eight pointer had shadowed and stared down several lesser bucks and I could tell by his walk that he was in a very aggressive mood. With three lesser bucks following him and the doe, the eight point began bluffing the bucks by making rubs. In all he made five rubs on trees over four inches in diameter before covering four hundred yards, and in each case he put a lot of physical effort into them. By his actions he was telling the other bucks to get lost. I've also seen similar behavior from dominant bucks as they tried to protect bedded estrous does from other bucks.

When November arrives in the north, chaos arrives in the whitetail's world. No doe is safe when bucks begin the chase phase of the rut.

When I photographed this buck making a rub, I wanted to depict movement, so I intentionally blurred the photo to help capture the mood of the moment.

Scraping

Over the last fifteen years I've studied and photographed the whitetail's scraping behavior, and with each passing year I've become more and more intrigued by this phenomenon. Like rubs, scrapes are signposts or markers that bucks leave throughout their territory to alert other deer of their presence. In a way they are like bus stops, and it's not uncommon for several bucks to use the same scrape if it is located in a high-use area. The beauty of this is that bucks establish a network of scrapes and regularly check them in their travels.

When a scrape is made, a buck is trying to leave as much of his scent as possible. In the process of making a scrape he rubs his preorbital and forehead glands, as well as salivating on the

With rutting in full swing, bucks make many rubs throughout their territory. Most are random rubs on small trees but in some areas big bucks will make line rubs like these.

This buck is truly the "bull of the woods." When this size tree is rubbed by a buck it can only be from a large mature animal. When a buck rubs a tree he's not only leaving his visual calling card but also leaving as much scent as possible by rubbing his nasal and forehead glands on the rub.

scrape's overhanging licking branch. He also paws away debris beneath the branch so he can urinate into the scrape's exposed earth. In the North a buck will usually splay his legs during the urination process, if the scrape is made prior to about October 25. After this time he'll begin to do what is called rub urination. This takes place when the buck places his hind legs together and urinates through his tarsal glands into the scrape while rubbing these glands together. By urinating through his tarsal glands a buck is able to leave even more of his scent.

How often will a buck make a scrape? Unfortunately research has shown that nearly 70 percent of all scraping activity takes place under the cover of darkness, so it's difficult to accurately determine. In spite of this I've been able to witness some interesting scraping behavior in the Adirondacks. Though scraping is not as frequent in September and early October, bucks will make many during this time. However, just prior to the full blown breeding time scraping kicks into high gear.

On October 26, 1994, I was able to observe or "shadow" a large buck for the entire day. During this time he only bedded for two of the ten hours of daylight, and was constantly on the move (for six straight hours at one point) searching for receptive does. The only time he stopped was when he would make a rub, scrape, bed for a few minutes, or listen to the sounds of the woods. The fewest number of scrapes he made in a given hour was five. The most was twelve. He literally worked every licking branch he encountered. Twice he came upon does and the chase began. Once I thought I lost the buck but after getting to a high

Bucks will make many scrapes in areas where there is a good buck to doe ratio. Where scrapes are located in heavy use areas, more than one buck will use the same scrape.

While most bucks keep their front feet on the ground while working a scrape's licking branch, I have observed on several occasions the kind of licking branch behavior shown here. Not only did this buck leave his scent at the normal level but also placed it higher on the branch.

After working the scrape's licking branch, a buck will remove all debris from under the licking branch by pawing the ground. It's this process that gives the scrape its name and is done to ready the scrape for the next step, which is the urination process.

After the licking branch has been worked and the ground pawed out, the buck places his tarsal glands together and rocks back and forth as he urinates into them. The excess urine falls from the tarsal glands into the scrape and leaves the buck's own distinct odor in the scrape. This aspect of scraping is called rub urination.

When a doe comes into estrus she attracts several bucks. Usually the larger more aggressive bucks bully and shadow the smaller bucks into leaving. In this case the two smaller bucks steered clear of the big mature buck as it approached with its ears pulled back and its hair standing on end. Such an appearance shows the lesser bucks what kind of attitude the dominant buck has.

point in the woods was able to hear him walking in the distance and rejoined him. During the course of the day he made only five rubs and encountered no other bucks while traveling. During ten years of keeping accurate records it's been my experience that a traveling buck (during the two weeks prior to the actual breeding) will make between five and twelve scrapes per hour.

Fight for Dominance

An aspect of whitetail behavior that intrigues all who love this animal is the way they determine dominance, or pecking order. During the antler growing process some bucks will attempt to dominate other bucks by fighting with their hooves.

When a big buck bullies two lesser bucks away from a hot doe, the smaller bucks often take their frustration out on each other in a heated sparring match. These can be much more ferocious than early season sparring matches; on several occasions I've seen them get very ugly.

Once the velvet is stripped from their antlers, bucks will begin sorting out who is boss by shadowing or sparring with each other. Shadowing usually amounts to one buck pulling his ears back and setting his hair on end in order to show another buck that he is one tough customer and not to be messed with.

Over the years I've photographed and observed many sparring matches between white-tailed bucks. In a true sense sparring is not fighting, though it may appear as such. A sparring match between two white-tailed bucks is like a friendly wrestling match; the two participants merely push and shove each other around. Sometimes these sparring matches last up to a half hour or more,

though most are reasonably brief. Like hoof fighting and shadowing, sparring is a way for bucks to sort out who is boss. However, there are times that none of these activities will work in determining who is king of the forest. When this happens drastic measures take place between bucks.

An aspect of whitetail behavior that is seldom seen is the knock-down, drag-out fight, a fight that takes the participants to the edge of death. When two equal size bucks find themselves on the range where competition is strong for the available doe population, fights to the death are a real possibility. In all my years of pursuing whitetails I've only seen three such fights. They don't last long but the action is fast and furious. It's an unforgettable expe-

When two mature bucks overlap each other's territories or find themselves in pursuit of the same doe, a fight to-the-death often ensues. I photographed this fight in far south Texas. Although it lasted only about five minutes I was sure one of the bucks would die. They threw each other around with ease, and during the fight there was much grunting and bawling. Such fights end when one of the bucks is seriously injured or the lesser buck breaks and runs off.

rience. The amount of noise generated by a true buck fight is incredible. Often one, or both, of the combatants sustains serious injury from the flurry of flashing antler tines. As Chapter 5 unfolds you'll be able to see a fight to the death and various other aspects of the rut unfold as one buck took on all comers for the right to breed a doe.

I came upon this buck shortly after he and another buck had finished a ferocious fight. The other buck ran when I approached, but this one couldn't. The buck had a large hole in his neck and stayed stationary for nearly twenty minutes. During this time I walked around the buck at a safe distance and burned several rolls of film of the wet, bloody-antlered buck. It's one of the most incredible things I've ever seen in the wild and illustrates the awesome power and exhaustion that such fights generate.

The day before I took this photo I observed this buck with a matching left antler. He didn't appear to be hurt but he had to have been in an incredible fight to have broken his antler beam off at the skull.

It's amazing how much punishment a buck can take in a fight and still survive. In spite of the buck's rear lower jaw being visible, the wound healed and he lived to see another autumn.

To me this is the essence of what autumn in whitetail country is all about.

CHA5TER

Fight for Dominance

As this photo essay will illustrate, a white-tailed doe creates a real five alarm fire in the woods when she starts to come into estrus. The scene is nothing short of incredible and the energy bucks expend for the right to breed a doe is phenomenal. During my thirty-plus years of pursuing northern whitetails as a hunter and photograph-er I've seen the white-tailed buck's fight for domi-nance and breeding rights played out so many times I've stopped counting. Since I began seriously pho-tographing whitetails in 1979 I've been fortunate to have filmed the inner workings of the whitetail's breeding six times from start to finish. What follows will provide insight into this fascinating part of a whitetail's yearly journey. I photographed this sequence over a two day period in early November not far from my home, in an area closed to hunting.

Early one morning I spotted a small group of does feeding on a hillside. Within the group was a yearling spike buck that showed a lot of interest in one of the does. Knowing the does would be coming into estrus any time, I watched intently as the spike chased the big doe around. By mid-morning his party was over. The doe was coming into estrus and the scent of her season began attracting a lot of attention.

As a big eight pointer came on the scene the spike backed off and the chase was on. For over ten minutes the big buck chased the doe through the hardwoods in hopes of breeding her. Because of the way she smelled, the buck no doubt wondered why the doe would not stop and stand for him. Little did he know that it would take another day of chasing before she would finally hit peak estrus and let him breed her.

A big eight point buck intimidates a spike buck as he moves toward a doe who is entering her estrous cycle.

The dominant eight point buck separates the estrous doe from the rest of the group, and the chase begins.

With the odor of a hot doe hanging heavy in the woods, buck activity began to increase. I was so intent on watching the eight pointer chase the doe that I didn't notice a small ten point moving in until he began grunting and challenging the big buck. For a second I thought there would be a fight. The two bucks stood ten yards apart, each waiting for the other to make a move. The eight point dragged out a series of low guttural grunts before snort wheezing at the small ten point. Figuring there was no way he was going to win a battle, the small ten pointer backed off and let the eight point take up the chase. And what a chase it was.

For over ten minutes the big grunting buck chased the doe through a swamp before running her through a pond not far from where I was set up with my camera. As I burned film I could see water flying in every direction as the buck tried to get her stopped. It was obvious the buck was becoming very frustrated and tired. From my vantage point on a hill above the pond I noticed a different, smaller buck moving past me through open hardwoods. I thought to myself, "Man, you don't have a clue what you're in for. I hope you have your armor on."

He didn't. As the big buck chased the doe toward the pond's edge the four point tried to join in the chase. It was a big mistake. Talk about near suicide! I thought the big eight point would gut the smaller buck right there on the bank before running him off. The big buck grunted loudly, almost like a bawl, turned around and looked across the pond. Entering the water was the small ten point the big buck had run off earlier. I had to give the small ten point credit for being persistent. When the ten point made it halfway across the pond the big buck began chasing him in an attempt to steer him away from the doe. Both bucks disappeared into the brush at the pond's edge.

As a smaller ten point buck follows the doe's hot scent to the scene, the big eight pointer breaks off the chase to stare him down.

After winning the stare-down with the ten pointer, the eight pointer chases the doe into a nearby swamp and pond.

The eight pointer is momentarily distracted by a four point buck. The big buck swiftly charges his small competitor, driving him from the scene.

At dawn on the second day, yet another buck intrudes on the eight pointer and the estrous doe. Within seconds, a loud, vicious fight erupts between the bucks.

I don't know what went on, but from the number of snort wheezes I heard there was a lot of anger being vented. While this was going on the doe took off on a dead run, fleeing into an alder swamp to the southwest. From my vantage point I could see that she made a big loop and headed in a northerly direction toward some hardwoods over five hundred yards away. What happened next impressed me as much as anything I've witnessed in nature.

When the big eight pointer emerged from the brush he stared around trying to locate the doe. He picked up her track at the pond's edge and began following it in the southwesterly direction the doe had gone. There was no way the buck could know that the doe had made a loop and was now due north from his present position. After following the track about a hundred yards the buck stopped, sniffed the air current coming out of the north, left the doe's track and took off on a dead run to where the doe was.

Rather than continuing to track the doe for another five hundred yards the buck was able to locate her from air currents. . . at over four hundred yards. Had I not seen this I never would have believed it. I now understand why bucks are able to detect estrous does from such great distances. With the light of the day vanishing, I caught up with the buck and doe as the first day ended.

Knowing the doe would probably not move far in the night, I was back in place as the next morning dawned. I was right. Though I'm sure there was rut-

ting activity in the night, the doe was within two hundred yards of where I saw her at the end of the previous day. As she browsed and ate grass next to a stream she periodically looked up into the woods, searching for the big eight point.

With the sun inching toward the horizon the big buck walked down through the woods and stopped on a logging road about fifty yards from the doe. In the distance I could see a deer walking down the road toward the buck. Through my camera lens I was able to tell it was a buck, but wasn't sure how big. The big eight pointer stared in the buck's direction as the distance between them narrowed. It was evident something was about to happen. When the

distance was cut to a few feet both bucks pulled their ears back and plowed into each other with tremendous force. For the next few minutes I witnessed the most ferocious fight I've ever seen between two bucks. The sound of antlers rattling and grinding pierced the fresh morning air. It was louder than any rattling sound I've ever heard. Bawling, moaning, and loud grunting provided background "music" for the rattling.

I quickly shot a roll of film and had to reload. In the process I missed an incredible photo, one forever etched in my mind. With me loading film and the two bucks locked up wrestling in the road, a four point (the same one from the day before) ran from the woods and plowed into the hind quarters of the big eight point's adversary. It didn't even phase the fighting buck.

In the midst of pushing and rattling the two bucks found themselves off the road in high swale

The battling bucks lock up and soon become tangled in swale grass. A smaller nine point buck approaches. It seems anxious to join the fight, but never engages.

After the eight pointer drives off the intruder, he makes a scrape as a show of dominance, and works a licking branch above it.

After hiding in thick evergreens for several hours, the estrous doe emerges from the thicket. The eight pointer, who was bedded nearby, stands up, moves toward the doe, and waits to breed her.

grass. Quickly they became entangled in the grass and couldn't move. The fight had now drawn a crowd. Surrounding the two fighting bucks were a spike, four point, the small ten point from the day before, and a nine point. The sound of antlers coming together and the smell of a hot doe had created the ultimate rutting party. The scene was electrifying.

Except for the sound of bucks breathing heavily and the ringing in my ears, silence had taken over. The four whitetail spectators stood motionless waiting for the two entangled bucks to make their next move. The big eight point gave out a loud moan and came to life. In one big thrust the big eight point pushed the intruding buck into the small stream, making a big *kerplunk* sound when he hit the water. The smaller nine point who had shown up only minutes before was now dancing around trying to

get in on the fight. The big eight point threw himself into the stream, trying to impale the water soaked buck. He missed his mark and rammed his antlers into the stream's bank. Before he could regain his balance the buck he had been fighting jumped up and ran off. The fight was over.

Exhausted, the big eight point stood motionless, trying to catch his breath. Blood dripped from his mouth and nose (see the photo that leads off this chapter) as he stared down the four bucks who had been attracted to the battle. It was enough to cause the crowd to disperse and each buck went in a different direction. After a few minutes the bloodied buck walked over to a scrape along the stream and worked the licking branch.

For nearly half an hour the buck stood at the stream's edge like a punch drunk fighter. His behavior suggested that he wasn't sure what was going on, though I'm sure he knew he'd just been through the fight of his life. Then as if on cue he lowered his head and began walking toward the woods. Within one hundred yards he found the estrous doe bedded in thick evergreens which were too thick for him to get his antlers through. For the next two hours the buck and doe played cat and mouse as the buck alternated between standing and bedding, while guarding the brush where the doe was hiding.

Around mid-morning the doe stood up, no longer able to contain the hormonal feeling within her, and moved from the evergreen sanctuary. The big eight point came up out of his bed grunting as the spectator bucks watched from a distance. This time the doe did not run. She stood and let the buck come up behind her, lick her flanks, and mount and breed her as the others watched. In less than a minute it was all over.

The buck continued to guard the doe for the rest of the day, allowing no one, buck or doe, to approach his lady friend. The next day I returned to find only the doe. She no longer "smelled right" so no one but her fawns were interested in her. The bucks were gone looking for another hot doe to harass.

During the two-day period I observed and photographed many profound things about the white-tail's rut, from the courting, to the chasing, to the fighting, to the breeding. It was an incredible experience. After seeing everything unfold it is easy to understand why bucks wind up with so many injuries. The literature says that on average a mature white-tailed buck will breed up to ten does in a given fall. If this is the case, I'm amazed that any survive the fray.

The buck mounts and breeds the doe after ensuring she is ready. In less than a minute, the entire sequence is complete.

CHAPTER 6

The Lure of Antlers

Nothing creates a "people jam" faster than the sight of a large racked white-tailed buck. This is evidenced by viewing people's reactions, be it at a hunting show or in the wild. Antlers simply transfix people. I'll never forget the first time I saw a large racked white-tailed buck on my parent's farm. I couldn't have been more than six years old but the memories of that big ten point loping in front of my dad's pickup have stayed with me for a lifetime. Antlers have a way of doing that to people. Ever since, I've been fascinated by all aspects of a whitetail's antlers, from the growth process to their various size and shapes. No two are alike and they're a testimony to the wonders of God's creation.

In most portions of North America few white-tailed bucks live long enough to reach their full antler growth potential. However, in areas where they do, antler size can be truly amazing. Several factors must come into play for a whitetail buck to be able to grow a large set of antlers. Nutrition, how the region is managed, genetics, and age all play a part. But with all things being equal, age is the critical ingredient for a white-tailed buck to grow a whopping size rack. For this to happen a buck needs to be at least three years of age. This is because during the first three years a buck's rapidly growing body is building bone and muscle tissue so nearly all of his nutritional intake is going to this end. Once he reaches three years of age his physical growth is complete. From this point on a buck's nutritional surplus goes to antler development.

The two photos that accompany this text illustrate what can happen if a buck is able to reach maturity. The first photo shows a New York Adirondack buck when it was a year-and-a-half old. The second photo was taken when he was six-and-a-half years

Antlers are what makes whitetails so majestic. These two bucks exemplify what mature bucks are all about; because their racks are very even they would be classified as typical racked bucks.

old and illustrates how a buck reaches full antler potential when nutrition, genetics, management, and age come together. Interestingly this buck's last three sets of antlers have been nearly identical.

Genetics determines whether a buck becomes a typical (uniform antlers) eight pointer or a twenty point non-typical (irregular antlers) when it reaches maturity. For this same reason some bucks have high narrow racks, some short-tined wide racks and others heavy multi-point antlers. Unfortunately, a buck must be able to reach maturity in order to see his genetic makeup. Though there are exceptions, once

I photographed this yearling buck in 1990 when it had its first set of antlers.

After surviving five years the same buck grew to be a beautiful big-racked buck and is testimony of what can happen when a buck is allowed to live to its full potential. Of all the ingredients required for growing large racked bucks, age is the key. Without age, large racks are not possible.

a buck reaches four or five years of age his rack will be very similar until he reaches about nine years old. Then, depending on the animal, his rack will begin to get smaller with age.

During the course of my seminars I'm often asked, "Is it true that if a buck is a spike when it's a-year-and-a-half old it will always be a spike?" Among authorities on whitetails this has been a hotly debated subject. Though my intent is not to add fuel to the fire I'll say this. It's been my experience that this simply is not the case. On several occasions I've photographed bucks whose first racks were spindly spikes only to see them develop a trophy class set of antlers by the time they were five years of age. The best example I've ever seen was of a buck that carried three inch spikes when he was one-and-a-half years old and turned into a large eight point at five-and-a-half. There are simply too many variables involved for the "once a spike always a spike" theory to be valid.

Another often-asked question is, "Why do whitetails grow antlers?" To my knowledge no one knows for sure—at least my experience and search of the literature turns up nothing. In my pursuit of whitetails I've heard all kinds of reasons why whitetails grow antlers. Probably the most frequently heard is, "bucks grow antlers to ward off predators." Though this might make sense it cannot be valid. If this were the case does would grow antlers. For another, a whitetail's antlers would need to stay on until the critical winter predation season is over. This assumption doesn't hold water because over 95% of all does do not grow antlers (some do) and for the most part a white-tailed buck sheds or casts his antlers from January to March each year (in the north), before winter has ended.

My feeling is that bucks grow antlers for dominance. This assumption makes sense if you think about it. Once a buck reaches maturity all the lesser bucks shy away from him for three reasons: his body size, his aggressiveness (attitude), and more importantly his antler size. And the bigger the antlers the worse a buck's attitude usually is. For these reasons his "equipment" says he's boss.

In early July when a mature buck's antlers are half grown he begins to bully other bucks in order to determine pecking order before autumn. All bucks realize that antler size determines rank so the fall's breeding rights are often determined beforehand. However, when two mature bucks' territory overlaps a confrontation often results during the fall for the breeding rights to the area's doe population. When these battles occur it's usually the bigger antlered buck that's victorious.

Also, scientists and keen whitetail observers believe that mature white-tailed does gravitate to the bigger bucks when they come into estrus. Whitetails are no different than humans in that they recognize each other by appearance and seem to have a preference for the more masculine looking bucks, especially those who wear their antlers like a crown. Throughout the hard antler season bucks and does immediately know each buck they encounter by the head gear they are wearing.

There is also another side to the whitetail's antler story. Antlers are truly magical to people, and because of this hunters love to hunt big-racked whitetails. There is nothing wrong with this, providing the hunters stay within the law. After all, man has been hunting for trophy animals since the dawn of time, with historical evidence such as pictographs bearing this out. Unfortunately we live in a world where everything is determined by records. Basketball, baseball, and football records flow off the tongues of nearly every male in American households. If you don't think so just ask a ten-year-old to recite what he knows about sports in America. I coached a little league baseball team for twenty years and was always amazed by the long list of statistics

Whether a white-tailed buck grows a typical or non-typical set of antlers is primarily determined by genetics. I photographed this non-typical racked buck in 1992. The photo that leads off this chapter is the same buck in 1993. As you can see, once a buck reaches maturity his rack is very similar from one year to the next.

those kids could rattle off. There is a similar record book mentality when it comes to white-tailed deer.

There needs to be some form of recordkeeping to determine the quality of a natural resource. The Boone & Crockett Club keeps such records. Antler collecting and the desire to have a big set of whitetail antlers have become big business in America. Though a record book for white-tailed deer is good there's an ugly spin-off from it. Because Boone & Crockett record-book size antlers can command thousands of dollars, greed has entered the special domain of the whitetail's world. With financial gain to be had, poaching is becoming an ugly problem wherever whitetails are found.

Let me illustrate. I live in some of the most productive whitetail country in North America. For years this area has had all but one of the ingredients for having mature white-tailed bucks. The one

Sometimes a buck's antlers will change their configuration over time, as is the case with these two photos. The first photo was taken in 1992, when the buck was a three year old. Two years later the same buck's antlers had become heavier and more typical. I nicknamed this buck "the Coke-can buck" because his antler bases were as big around as Coke cans.

Drop-tined bucks are prized by hunters and are believed to be a genetic trait. In spite of this there is no guarantee that the drop tine will repeat from one year to the next.

exception was that landowners and hunters did not allow bucks to grow to maturity. Whitetails and the sight of them are loved by nearly all the people who live in our region. So, during the last five years many surrounding landowners have formed a Quality Deer Management chapter in an attempt to grow a quality deer herd (as opposed to the quantity deer herd we've always had) in our area. The efforts have been phenomenal and the sight of

mature deer on the land has given the locals many rewarding experiences.

Unfortunately it has also caused greed's ugly head to surface here in rural America. Last fall four headless carcasses from mature bucks were found in our county. Then, on the eve of deer season a fifth buck was recovered before the poacher could remove the buck's rack. It carried a huge set of antlers. Sadly the perpetrator has not been found. Was this person

This buck is a beautiful example of how big a white-tailed buck can grow. He was eventually killed by a hunter, and his heavy symmetrical rack scored 172 under the Boone & Crockett Club's typical scoring category.

Next to non-typical racks, whitetail enthusiasts love seeing wide-racked bucks. I photographed this buck on a large ranch in south Texas. It has the widest inside spread of any whitetail I've seen. Interestingly, it was just an average racked two-and-a-half year old when I first photographed it in 1989. He's as close to a 26" inside spread as you'll ever see.

a hunter? Certainly not. He was nothing more than a thief, and in my opinion a very sick person. You might ask, "What would cause someone to do such a terrible thing?" It's anyone's guess, but probably money or the bragging rights associated with killing a record book buck had a lot to do with it. Unfortunately, poaching, like dealing drugs or stealing for a living, is but one more by-product of a society headed in the wrong direction. And as long as there is so much emphasis on record book whitetails, the problem will persist.

This buck is the epitome of what big bucks and antlers are all about. He had an incredibly bad attitude and was as aggressive as any buck I've ever seen.

No two sets of whitetail antlers are ever alike. Both of these bucks are basically ten pointers, but the one on the left is much heavier and larger. It's not uncommon for bucks like this to travel together during non-rutting months.

CHA7PTER

Deer at Rest

What's the most frequent whitetail behavior? It may come as a surprise to some but it's bedding and everything associated with a whitetail's resting time. On average a whitetail beds a whopping 70% of the day. This is only an average, and the 70% figure does not apply throughout the year. In the dead of winter (in the north) whitetails literally go to the edge of hibernation and may bed most of the time. On the other hand lactating does and rutting bucks may bed far less, so the 70% figure is a rough year-around average.

Bedding and Terrain

Although I've spent my entire life in whitetail country, the whitetail's use of terrain when bedded never ceases to amaze me. Perhaps it shouldn't; after all, they are the ultimate survival machine. But the way they work the wind when bedded leaves me with a great deal of respect for them. Usually they tend to bed with their back to the wind. There are no wasted senses with whitetails, and by bedding in this manner they can use their eyes to see downwind and their sense of smell to alert them of upwind danger. In hilly country they also have a tendency to bed just over the edge of a ridge if the wind is blowing downhill. This allows them to see below and smell their intruder before it sees them.

In many ways they are like people in that they prefer to bed in the same location over and over. On more than one occasion I've seen bucks and does bed, get up to feed, and come right back to

Whitetails will occasionally stretch out their entire length when bedded. This buck even appeared to lapse into sleep with his eyes slightly rolled but open. This is the only time I've ever seen this happen. At first I thought the buck was dead, but then it snapped up its head, yawned, and closed it eyes for twenty seconds.

Depending on air temperatures, individual deer, and how weary it becomes, a deer will rest its head in various positions when it dozes or sleeps. When temperatures are warm, the head is seldom tucked into the body, but in colder weather, the head will often slide alongside the body.

the bed they left. I've also observed whitetails bedding in the same place day after day and month after month. When it comes to bedding they are definitely creatures of habit.

Sleep

How whitetails sleep is a bit of a mystery. Little has been written on the subject but one thing is certain, they don't sleep like humans do. They doze for brief periods of time and seldom go into a deep sleep like people.

Perhaps the person most familiar with the subject is Cornell University Professor Aaron Moen. Moen is no stranger to whitetail enthusiasts, and is one of America's foremost deer researchers. Over the years Moen has conducted extensive research

dealing with the heart rates of whitetails as they relate to various stimuli and activities.

In Moen's research he refers to a point at which whitetails idle, like an engine idles, and uses the term "idling" when talking about a whitetail's heart rate when they bed or stand. A whitetail's average heart rate over a year's time when bedded is 72 beats per minute and 86 beats per minute when standing. When a whitetail walks and runs, the heart rate averaged over a year's time is 102 and 155 beats per minute respectively. So, in the absence of research one can assume that whitetails are probably building back cells when they are idling, while bedded or standing, and don't need to sleep like humans to build back cells.

Personally I've observed and photographed

Bucks will also spar while bedded. In this case a frisky spike buck pokes his head between the beams of a seven pointer and tussles with him. The seven pointer tolerated him for a bit, but then stood and drove him off with a kick.

several different kinds of whitetail behavior that appeared to be sleeping behavior. The most common kind of sleeping behavior I've seen is what researchers refer to as dozing. When this happens a deer's head can be either upright or tucked against its body. The deer will close his eyes (all or part of the way), and in some cases his head will start to bob, like a dozing person's would. On other occasions a deer's head will gradually move up and back with his nose pointing to the sky when he dozes. Also, temperature often dictates whether a deer curls up and tucks his head between his legs (cold weather) or keeps his head upright (warmer conditions) when bedded.

Though rarely, I've seen and photographed what I definitely thought was deep sleep. Once I observed a buck that bedded in the normal man-

ner, with his head up. After a few minutes his head began to bob. The buck then stretched his entire body on the ground, like he was dead. After watching him lay motionless for thirty minutes I tried to sneak up on the buck. I was able to get within fifteen yards before he came to and jumped up. The amazing thing about the whole situation was that the buck apparently had his eyes open the whole time. At least when I snapped off several photos his eyes were open, as the accompanying photo shows. Was he sleeping? I definitely feel he was, otherwise I never would have been able to sneak up on him like I did. This was one of the best examples of deep sleep I've ever seen, although I've witnessed others nearly as good.

Last winter I photographed a buck that was certainly close to hibernation and deep sleep. Even though the weather was sunny the wind chill was below zero when the buck bedded on the side of a hill around 1:00 P.M. Fifteen minutes after bedding, the buck curled up into a ball and stayed that way for over an hour before picking his head back up. Then, after about a minute, he returned to the curled up position. I'm not sure how long he stayed like this because I left the area before he moved again.

Alertness

How whitetails react to various stimuli around them is fascinating, especially when they are bedded. Time after time I've watched bedded whitetails go from dozing or sleeping to "red alert" in a heartbeat. This merely affirms how acute their senses are and how difficult they are to approach when they're bedded.

Last fall I was watching a bedded buck from a short distance. As he dozed he chewed his cud and his head kept bobbing up and down. Through my camera lens it looked as though he was hardly breathing as he burned time. Then, as if shot out of a cannon, the buck jumped to his feet and became very alert. I couldn't figure out what he was disturbed about, and from my vantage point I could see nothing. Within seconds a domestic dog came walking through the woods. Though the buck never ran (he let the dog pass by without detecting him) his side appeared to be heaving from his increased heart rate. The buck was obviously quite frightened. On other occasions I've seen similar examples of bedded deer dozing one second and fully alert the next.

The sparring between these two bucks is low-key. Note that the bedded buck appears calm and even has his eyes closed.

Does with young fawns often nurse and groom their offspring while bedded. If you ever see this in the wild, you'll never forget the sight. There is nothing more precious than a newborn fawn snuggling up to a bedded doe's nipples while the doe grooms it.

In 1978 Aaron Moen was involved in a study to determine heart rates of white-tailed deer fawns in response to recorded wolf howls. The test's results illustrate how quickly a whitetail can go from idling (sleeping) to full alert. In one test a bedded fawn's heart rate was 198 beats per minute fourteen seconds into the wolf howl. At this point the grass near the bedded fawn was deliberately rustled. The fawn jumped to its feet and the next readable heart rate, taken four seconds later, was 297 beats per minute. No doubt the fawn was a basket case from fright. The fawn's reactions illustrate what various stimuli do to whitetails.

Whitetails are very much aware of all that goes on around them when they are bedded, whether they are chewing their cud or dozing. It's been my experience that foreign sounds put them on alert in a second and they can easily differentiate between the footsteps of man and animal. So, just because deer are bedded and resting doesn't mean their guard is down. Just the opposite is true. When bedded they are more in tune with what is going on around them.

Over the years there have been articles written about hunters sneaking up on sleeping bucks and killing them before they wake up. No doubt this occasionally happens, but after years of in-the-woods observations I view such accounts as extremely rare. Conditions must be perfect for this to work.

Bedding Behavior

Because whitetails are ruminants they are capable of quickly eating substantial quantities of food and swallowing before it has a chance to be fully

Whitetails often groom themselves and each other while bedded. Grooming is more common when doe groups bed together, but bucks will also groom each other.

broken down. Once they devour their quick meal they move to their bedding area where they regurgitate it and chew their cud in order to get the food into a digestible form. Being able to handle their food at a later time enables them to stay out of harm's way, be it from natural predators or man.

In addition to chewing their cud and dozing, whitetails exhibit many different forms of behavior from ground level. Probably one of the most frequent things they do is groom. Whitetails use this resting time to bathe by licking themselves. Many times I've seen deer spend up to an hour just licking their legs and body. Often they will groom while their eyes are closed and they appear to be dozing. Also, other deer, particularly doe groups, will groom one another when bedded.

I'm of the opinion that subordinate bucks do a fair amount of sparring in the bedding area, although few have witnessed it. This usually takes place when one buck is bedded and another is moving around. In a recent fall I photographed one sequence that was particularly humorous. A seven point was bedded under an evergreen when a sublegal spike came by. The spike was obviously feeling his oats because he immediately began sparring with the seven point. Because he had no rack (for all practical purposes) the spike was able to get his head inside the seven point's antlers. The sparring went on for over fifteen minutes before the seven point got irritated, jumped up from his bed, and whacked the spike with his hoof, causing the spike to run off. I've photographed similar behavior before, and nearly every time it's the smaller buck that begins the sparring session with the bigger bedded buck.

During the rut, bedded does nearing estrus give aggressive bucks all kinds of fits. Before she is ready to breed a doe will flee the advances of a

buck by bedding in extremely thick cover. This usually amounts to a location where a buck cannot get his antlers through. It's an incredible thing to watch because the buck will be standing, often stomping his feet to show his frustration, while the doe hides nearby in thick cover. Of course when the doe comes into estrus she will be more cooperative and move from the thick cover to allow the breeding to take place.

Bedded does nursing their fawns is another behavior I've observed in the woods. If you ever have the opportunity of seeing it you'll never forget the sight. There's nothing more precious than to see a newborn snuggle up to a bedded doe's nipples and nurse while the doe grooms it.

The length of time a whitetail beds depends on the animal and a host of factors. Things like age, time of year, weather, and predator pressure are a few things that make up the equation. But on average few deer will bed longer than two hours at a time before standing up to at least stretch. Two exceptions to this are during the winter months in the north and during the rut. In the winter a deer may bed for longer periods of time and during the rut bedding may be brief for rut crazed bucks. After two hours deer will often stand, stretch and bed again in the same place. Other times they will walk anywhere from a few yards to several hundred yards before bedding again.

Regardless of the amount of time they spend bedding, whitetails have four active periods during the day. This activity is brought on by the normal rhythms of each individual animal. Generally this activity occurs around sunrise, midday, sunset, and midnight. However, whitetails do not operate by our clock, and a given animal's four active periods could be at most any time.

During the rut an estrous doe dictates when and where a buck goes. He will bed as long as she beds and move only when she chooses to do so.

A whitetail beds for two reasons, to rest and to be in a better position to survive. For the most part they know they are in danger every time they begin to move. Consequently they spend the majority of their day bedded. Rest is a fascinating aspect of whitetail behavior seldom observed. From birth, deer learn to live and survive by keeping a low profile in the cozy confines of their bedding area. It's here that they chew, doze, groom, and pass the day away as they struggle to witness another sunrise.

Deer, especially in colder climates, will curl into a ball while bedded to conserve energy.

CHA8TER

The Testing Time

The woods were dead silent as I made my way through snow laden hemlocks. Only the swish, swish, swish sound of my snow-shoe gliding through the snow could be heard. For the better part of an hour I had been cruising our property to assess how the deer were doing. As I crested a small knoll a deer jumped up from its bedding place under a spruce tree. I hurried my pace to get a glimpse of it. As I rounded the tree I was greeted with a pathetic sight. An eight-month-old fawn stood motionless, not twenty yards away, staring at me. I could tell from its tattered fur that it was in trouble. Within seconds it struggled to get away in the chest-deep snow.

As I write these lines we are in the throes of the worst winter in twenty-five years, perhaps ever. And

Nothing takes a greater toll on the whitetail than northern winters. The stress on this doe and fawn are evident by their appearance.

When the cold and snow of winter arrive, bucks, does and fawns begin shifting to their winter range. In some portions of North America this can be over a twenty-mile migration.

this is on the heels of the worst mast/apple crop in recent memory. Twenty inches of heavy white stuff came on November 15 and conditions have gotten progressively worse. I just heard the local meteorologist say on the radio that it has snowed forty-seven of the last fifty-nine days. Unfortunately, there's over sixty days of winter left.

Throughout the northern portion of the whitetail's range the above scenario is played out some

place every year. While it's happening you swear that there is no way any whitetails can survive nature's dose of cold and deep snow. But somehow most deer figure out a way to make it through to spring's green-up. Every time I think about what a whitetail must go through I'm in awe of their resilience and will to live another day.

When the last hope of autumn fades and cold and snowy days arrive on a regular basis, whitetails

With shorter days and a drop in testosterone levels, bucks begin tolerating each other for the first time since their bachelor groups broke up in September.

begin preparing for the coming endurance test. Oh, this isn't as man would think of it, they don't make lists or come up with any well-thought-out plan. They just know when it's time to make their move. In the remote areas, like New York's Adirondack Mountains or Maine's famed Allagash Region, whitetails begin migrating to their familiar winter-

ing areas when the heavy snows begin. Such locations are usually large conifer swamps, areas that offer protection against winter's cold. I've witnessed a migratory movement several times in the Adirondacks and each time it impresses me a little more. These migrations are something generations of whitetails have passed along to their young, with

each succeeding generation passing the ritual on to their offspring. Scientists refer to this behavior as yarding and without it happening deer would never be able to survive where harsh wilderness conditions exist. When whitetails yard in thick conifer swamps they do so to conserve energy and protect themselves against predators.

In farm country it's a different story. For the most part there is little or no migration. About the only thing that even resembles a migration takes place when the local herd moves off a north-facing range onto south-facing locations. This usually results in little more than a two or three mile shift.

I took this photo in mid-January. Even though the rut is but a faint memory, white-tailed bucks continue to work old scrapes' licking branches throughout the winter months, even after they've cast their antlers.

Even during the storms of winter, bucks still make an effort to smell an old rub for other bucks' scent.

But in both cases a whitetail's response to winter is nearly the same.

In most northern regions winter's fury is released in December, during the shortest period of daylight. This causes some distinct biological shifts in a whitetail's body. With less daylight and the testosterone level dropping, whitetail bucks become less and less aggressive. This along with range condition, nutrition, and health of a given buck will have a lot to do with when he drops his antlers. In most northern climates the casting or shedding of antlers takes place from December to March. The literature suggests that the older, more mature bucks drop their antlers first. I've found this to be the case where rut-worn bucks inhabit an area of marginal food sources. However, in locations where food was abundant I've seen trophy class bucks carry their antlers into late February.

Another biological shift within all whitetails

On warmer winter days bucks will revert to their September behaviors and spar with each other. These observations have led me to believe that this is mostly a conditioned behavior, but it is also a way for individual bucks to set up their pecking order.

When whitetails move to winter ranges some interesting photo ops take place. Look close. There are six trophy bucks woven into this forest setting. Can you find all the members of this bachelor group?

occurs as they adjust to winter. During the early part of winter they have reduced thyroid function and decreased metabolic activity. This results in less food being needed for survival. Then by mid-winter their system slows down even further and they enter a time when they are almost hibernating on the hoof. Scientists refer to this as a semi-hibernating state. It allows deer to become quite resistant to nutritional deprivation and the stresses of winter's harsh climate. This phenomenon reduces a deer's food intake by approximately 30%, regardless of the food available, and their activity by up to 50%.

The downside of their movement reduction is that they become very reluctant to move from a given location to another to find food when they go into semi-hibernation. I've seen this behavior exhibited often when I've gone into a particular wintering area to cut browse. During tough winters I've had to cut trees within three hundred yards of where the deer were bedding just to get them interested in the new cache of food. Other times I've seen them half a mile from very good browse and not desirous enough to look for it. It's almost like the food had to be right under their nose. This complicates matters because during the winter months they need at least six pounds of browse a day to survive. And if they don't move to look for food their condition deteriorates quickly.

If whitetails happen to winter where the habitat has been damaged or good food is not present their condition goes downhill quickly. For this reason it's important that they winter where the more nutritional foods are. In the Northeast, browse like sumac, red maple, basswood, apple, white ash,

Any time whitetails are forced to run during the winter months, they burn energy they cannot afford to spend. This kind of stress takes a heavy toll on deer whenever it happens.

During periods of severe cold, feeding can be sporadic. When whitetails do feed, however, they require six to ten pounds of browse a day. I photographed these mature bucks feeding on a downed tree in late January.

Corn is a high energy food, and any standing corn field will be ravaged if whitetails can find it during the winter months.

Whether bedded or standing, whitetails go into "semi-hibernation" when the snow and severe cold of winter sets in.

When the heavy snows arrive, bedding becomes the primary winter behavior. In some areas whitetails will be bedded over 90% of the time during the dead of winter.

white cedar, and hemlock are preferred foods and vital for a herd's survival. When whitetails begin feeding on non-preferred foods like American beech it's an indication they are in trouble.

Though whitetails are very sluggish during the winter months they can be very aggressive when it comes to food. Many times while photographing I've seen deer fight each other for food, or guard a given source of browse they've found. Such displays are not pretty sights, especially when a doe com-

Look closely at this photo. On the left is a yearling spike buck with one-inch antlers. On the right is a fawn button buck. The spike picked a fight with the fawn and wound up getting beat by the aggressive youngster.

When a buck's testosterone level bottoms out he sheds his antlers.

petes with her fawns for food. Winter truly is a time of survival of the fittest and at times deer appear to be saying, "it's everyone for themselves, and if you want to eat you'll have to fight for it."

As mentioned in the chapter's opening, this winter has been brutal on wildlife here in the Northeast. Not too many days ago I watched a doe dig through two feet of snow covering a clover field in her search for food. It was pathetic. She must have made a hundred strokes with her hooves just to get to ground level. With snow piled on each side of the hole she tried to get a little nourishment from the few blades of frozen clover she uncovered. The bottom line was that the doe expended more energy getting to the food than she got from what she ate. Unfortunately this story is played out more than anyone realizes during the winter months.

As the previous chapter details, whitetails bed for extended periods of time during the winter months. However, if a warm-up occurs they are much more active. For the most part they limit their movement to the middle of the day during this time. When movement exists bucks and does often socialize with other deer around them. Does spend time grooming their fawns, and bucks, which have reformed their pre-rut bachelor groups, tend to spend time grooming, rubbing, sparring (if they still have antlers), and on occasion working overhanging licking branches. If one or both of the bucks have lost their antlers a sparring match can be very humorous during this time. Once while photographing in an Adirondack deer yard I observed a big bodied buck (who had shed his antlers) attempt to spar with a medium-size ten-point. The buck without antlers gingerly tried to place his forehead between the burrs of the other buck's antlers and push. It was kind of like watching a tug boat push a barge around. He had the right idea but didn't have the equipment to get the job done. I've also watched antlerless bucks attempt to rub trees. Once the warm up ends and the cold returns, the fun and games are over and deer revert to more dormant behavior.

The predator's role in managing whitetail numbers is very controversial, especially when it comes to winter-stressed deer. Much of the literature states that coyotes do not have a significant impact on whitetail populations. However, some of the best biologists are rethinking this. Coyotes and wolves are very opportunistic and arguably the best hunters on the continent. In the farm country I call home, coyotes definitely have an impact on our winter deer herd but nothing like in the remote regions where snow packs are significant. When assessing impact it's important to realize that it doesn't mean that a predator has to actually kill a deer, though

this does happen. As Aaron Moen's research shows, whitetails can be stressed by the mere presence of predators. Such stress is cumulative and impacts the deer herd. By winter's end everything adds up and too often the end result is not in the whitetail's favor.

But as with all seasons, winter ends and gives way to spring. The yearly cycle is complete and once again the whitetail looks to the future and the hope of warmer, sunnier days.

Predation in the white-tailed herd can be significant during the winter months. Winter is not kind to deer. When deep crusty snow prevails, domestic dogs, coyotes and wolves thrive on whitetails.

Behind the Camera

It's hard to say when the photography bug first bit me. Certainly the seeds were planted when I began admiring Leonard Lee Rue's and Erwin Bauer's whitetail photos while I was in high school. Both were true pioneers in wildlife photography. I couldn't help but wonder what it would be like to get images like theirs. Because of their inspiration I bought my first 35mm camera, a top-of-the-line Miranda Sensorex, while stationed in Vietnam in the late 1960s. While there I was fortunate to be on a

base where there was a photo hobby shop. The shop had the capability of both color and black and white processing, and during my fourteen months in Southeast Asia I shot and developed my own film on a regular basis. Because many of the military photographers used the shop to process their film I was able to get tips and learn from their work. When I returned from Vietnam in 1970, I had one camera body and a 200mm lens, and was determined to begin photographing nature.

Quickly I realized that the 200mm lens was not long enough to get the whitetail photos I wanted, so I bought a cheap 400mm f5.6 lens. Though inferior

Good clean portraits of whitetails can be great if they are put in a beautiful setting.

Though the previous photo is fine, portraits can be improved by moving the subject off center, as this and the photo leading off the chapter illustrate. Doing so gives the picture more impact.

to today's lenses it gave me a start. With it in hand I frequently photographed in a local deer wintering area during my first year home. The experience hooked me.

As I discovered in January of 1970, the beauty of hunting deer with a camera is that the season lasts all year and there are no bag limits. I shoot Nikon cameras and lenses and presently rely heavily on three lenses; a 35-70mm f2.8, an 80-200 f2.8 ED zoom and a 200-400 f4 ED zoom. These lenses are extremely sharp (and expensive!), and allow me to photograph when the light is less than adequate. I always try to use the 80-200 zoom mounted on a tripod or camera gun-stock, though I will shoot it off-hand if lighting permits. The 200-400 zoom is heavy and is always used with a tripod, to ensure that the pictures are as sharp as possible.

Whenever I'm photographing animals I try to improve on the photos I take of them. One way to accomplish this is to make the deer a part of a scenic. This photo and the following spread were done in this way and capture the essence of what whitetail country is all about.

The color film I use changes with technology. For years I shot primarily with Kodachrome 64. When the "film wars" heated up the film got better and better and caused me to go with what I perceived to be the best at any given time. As a result I presently use three color slide films: Fuji Velvia (ASA 50) for scenics, Fuji 100 Provia (ASA 100) for animals, and Kodachrome 200 for dim light situations. I use Fuji Velvia for scenics because it's one of the sharpest films made and its colors are incredible. I shoot it at its ASA rating of 50. Fuji Provia is nearly as sharp as Velvia and I shoot it at an ASA of 125, even though it is ASA

Whenever I take portraits of people or animals I focus on their eyes. The eye is the center of attention and reveals the soul and character of the subject. Also, the glint of the eye adds to the overall photo.

100 film. Kodachrome 200, an ASA 200 film, is sharp for a fast speed film and I shoot it at ASA 320 for better color saturation. Even though I shoot it at ASA 320 I do not tell the processing lab that I push it, I have them develop it normally.

As far as film is concerned, remember a couple of things. First, always shoot slide film. In most cases better prints can be made from slides than with print film and you'll have the slides for projection purposes, and if you are fortunate, for possible magazine sales. Second, the slower ASA film will be sharper and have better colors. Unfortunately, everything is a trade-off, and using slow speed film usually means shooting off a tripod.

Equipment

Today's cameras are vastly different than when I began photographing in the late '60s. Except for the light meter my first camera was an all manual 35mm. Today several of my cameras are capable of autofocus, can advance the film at over four frames per second, offer several programming modes, and have outstanding metering systems. They are truly state of the art. Because of this it's no wonder that many amateurs are able to get the outstanding photos they do. The nature of whitetail photography dictates that the 35mm camera is the format of choice. I also own several medium-format cameras and they are simply too big and bulky to get most wildlife photos.

Whenever someone asks me about what camera I'd recommend for photographing whitetails, I ask them how much money they are willing to spend. Today's cameras are not cheap. The more bells and whistles they have, the more costly they are. For the novice to serious amateur I recommend a medium priced 35mm camera body (with a good self timer built in) and a zoom lens in the 35-70mm range. This lens has a magnification of wide angle to about one and one quarter power and is excellent for scenics (note that the lens' magnification can be calculated by dividing 50 into the lens' millimeter). Most of today's medium priced camera bodies are as good as the top-of-the-line models of ten years ago and have excellent light meters and often auto-focus features. They also have built-in autowinders, which many refer to as motor drives. These can be good and bad. The good side is that the winder automatically advances the film so you can get to the next frame before the action changes. The bad side is the noise they make. Winder noise is foreign to whitetails and often spooks them. So, try to find a camera with a quiet autowinder.

In order to get started photographing deer a zoom lens in the 80-200mm range is essential. Also, it's best to get one with the lowest "f" setting you can afford. I have two 80-200 lenses that are f2.8s and they allow me to photograph in dim light (the smaller the "f" number the less light required to take a picture). People often think most deer photos are taken with long lenses. Though many are, the 80-200 is my workhorse lens and favorite when it comes to whitetails.

For the person serious about photographing whitetails, a 300mm, or better yet, a 400mm is a must for photographing the hard to approach animals. A 300mm (6 power) and 400mm (8 power) allow you to bring the animal in close without spooking it. In most instances the deer photographs that grace the covers of major nature magazines are taken with 300, 400, or 500mm lenses. The downside of these lenses are their weight and cost. The weight of most requires the use of a tripod. And the sticker price on these lenses can make a person cry or tremble, depending on his or her frame of mind. At today's prices one can expect to pay anywhere from $500 for a long telephoto to over $5,000 for a top-of-the-line model. As with the other lenses, the lower the "f" setting the better your chances of photography in dim light. The lower "f" setting lenses will also be the most expensive.

Light is the key to nature photography. For this reason I attempt to photograph in dramatic light, as this and the previous photo show. Getting this kind of lighting often means forethought and planning.

Stopping the action in fading light is not always easy, especially with relatively slow film in the camera. Bucks making rubs require at least a 250th of a second shutter speed. Fortunately I had just enough light to allow me to shoot at this speed and get the photo.

A sturdy tripod is one of the last pieces of equipment required to get into deer photography. Even though it's the last piece of equipment I mention, don't try to skimp on price as the quality of your photos will be in direct proportion to how steady the camera is when the photo is taken. My lightweight tripod is a Gitzo 226 with a Slik Pro ball head. My serious tripod, the one I use for my long lenses, is a Gitzo 320 with an ARCA ball head. This tripod is sturdy and heavy, but well worth the inconvenience of carrying it around.

One piece of equipment that isn't necessary but nice to have for whitetail photography is a portable blind. You can either make your own or purchase one of the many on the market. Dollar for dollar, Leonard Lee Rue's Ultimate Blind is hard to beat. Rue's blind is lightweight and can be put in place in less than a minute. I've spent too many hours to count in this blind and have taken some great photos with it.

Getting the Photo

When I began photographing deer I was more intent on just getting the deer in the frame than thinking about composition, depth of field, or lighting. All these aspects of photography take time to develop, but with a little knowledge the learning curve can be shortened. When composing whitetails, or any wildlife for that matter, I try to think how the subject will look best in the picture. Therefore I often

This photo was made possible with "photography deer lure," commonly known as shelled corn. By placing the bait where I wanted it I was able to get two bucks in action as they fought over breakfast.

put the subject off center in the picture so it becomes a part of the scene. In order to enhance the photo's composition I'll try to find a tree or some other object to frame the animal. From an artistic standpoint these things make the photos much better. To put it another way, I prefer to have my photos tell a story. This is not to say that I don't like to take tight portraits, because I do, but when the opportunity presents itself I try to get artistic.

Whenever I take portraits of people or animals I focus on their eyes. The eye is the center of attention and reveals the soul and character of the subject. Also, the glint of the eye adds to the overall photo. In addition I like to take these photos from the subject's eye level. If it's a fawn lying on the forest floor it means photographing from your belly.

Light is the key to whitetail photography and when possible I try to position the deer so they will

Luring whitetails within camera range is possible with decoys. Over the years I've been able to get many spectacular photos using decoys to fool bucks and does.

With the aid of a decoy I was able to illustrate the power and aggression of this buck. It's one of my most spectacular decoy images.

not be in direct sunlight. If I have a choice I'll opt to photograph the subject in cross or back light whenever possible. This kind of lighting makes for more dramatic photos. Getting this kind of lighting often requires forethought and planning.

My best photos usually occur when I go back to a location several times. During the course of photographing I constantly survey the scene to see which location will give the best photos when the sun shines. Because baiting is allowed in all the locations I photograph I preplan where I'll place the bait to get deer in the right position for the photos I want. I'll also "set the deer up" for certain photos. The accompanying photo of two bucks fighting was achieved by baiting.

Stopping a white-tailed buck in mid-flight is no easy task. This photo and the one on the back cover are two of a series. To freeze the action I shot at a shutter speed of a 500th of a second (Kodachrome 64 film), at f2.8, with my camera mounted on a gun stock.

At certain times I like to show motion in my photos. In this case I wanted to show movement in the snowflakes so I intentionally took the photo with a slow shutter speed.

Baiting can take on many forms and it's wise to find out if it is legal where you live. I learned a long time ago that the fastest way to whitetail action is through its belly. As a result I use apples and corn to lure deer within camera range. I also use one other device....a deer decoy. In the fall of the year white-tailed bucks respond well to a doe or buck decoy, especially during the mating season. I've used decoys extensively and had some incredible experiences with them. If you want to try "deercoying" it's important that the buck can spot the decoy, so placing it in an open area is a must. Also, make sure that the decoy is anchored to the ground. When a buck approaches a decoy he often becomes very aggressive and if the fake deer isn't anchored it may often get knocked over, and prematurely end the shoot. A word of caution is in order, however. Never use a decoy where hunting is permitted. Today's decoys are works of art and very authentic. As a result, from a distance hunters will seldom be able to tell the decoy from the real thing. So, always be safety conscious when using a decoy.

Perhaps the greatest challenge in nature photography is capturing the action. Things happen fast in the wild, and getting it right doesn't just happen. In order to stop action you need to shoot a shutter speed of at least a 500th of a second, or 1,000th of a second if you have enough light. Of course, there will be times when you want to show action by blurring the motion. The accompanying photo of a jumping buck and the one on the back cover were taken when I had two friends push a small woodlot for me. I positioned myself behind a large oak tree and waited for the action to unfold. Not long after they entered the woodlot, a doe came bounding right at me and jumped a deadfall. Though I did not take a photo of her I did get my bearings by focusing on her as she jumped. Fifty yards behind her was this buck. Because I was already focused on where the doe jumped, I was ready and took four frames through my motordriven camera (Kodachrome 64 film, 500th of a second, lens at f2.8) when he jumped the dead fall. Two of the four photos came out sharp. The key to these photos was realizing that the buck would follow the doe, knowing my equipment, and being ready when the moment of truth came. I guess some would call it luck. I call it taking advantage of the situation. . . and this is one of the big keys to whitetail photography. Knowing whitetail behavior and when to expect it has resulted in some incredible photos for me down through the years.

Creating a sense of motion is another way I like to tell the whitetail story. If snow is in the air and I want to depict it, I accomplish this by setting my shutter speed dial to a 60th of a second in order to show motion in the flakes. In the accompanying photo had I used any faster shutter speed, like 125th or 250th of a second, the snow would not have blurred as I wanted it to.

Where to Photograph

I do a great deal of whitetail photography on our farm and have many bait and blind locations right on our "back 40." However, my best photos come from areas where hunting is limited or prohibited. Many photographers photograph in deer pens, which are found throughout the United States. Though I've occasionally done this, my photos have not been that good because deer found in such enclosures are usually not photogenic. When I first began I relied on photographing in deer wintering areas. Though I still do this I also photograph on big estates, ranches, national parks (like Smoky Mountain National Park, where deer are used to people), and around metropolitan areas where hunting is limited or prohibited. The latter were unheard of twenty years ago but with urban sprawl are now quite common. Today, zoning regulations often make hunting limited and in such places the photo opportunities can be very good, though cropping cars and houses out of the pictures is a challenge.

Always be ready for action. To make sure I got this rutting action I had the camera's shutter set at a 500th of a second.

CHAPTER 10

2000 and Beyond

Reflecting back on my life, I think of a quieter, less complicated time. When I was a kid back in the early 1950s the technology of today wasn't even a vision on the horizon. There were no big supermarkets, no four-lane highways, and very few homes had television sets. The area of western New York I called home was made up of potato and dairy farms and miles and miles of dirt roads. For me having a good time meant going swimming in the nearby river, walking the railroad tracks to town to play baseball, hunting woodchucks on my parent's farm, or observing the white-tailed deer that were abundant in our area. By today's standards all these things probably seem backwoodsy to America's urban masses.

Access to private land will become a critical issue in dealing with future whitetail populations.

As we move into the next century this scene will become more and more common as urban sprawl moves into whitetail country.

One of the great whitetail challenges will be understanding the value of the resource.

But for me, growing up roaming my parents' back 40 was very special. In many ways it gave me a foundation for the values and ideas I have today. Part of this foundation was based on a sound work ethic and a keen understanding of the word *stewardship*. My farm community was made up of rugged individuals who toiled long and hard in the fields to make a living. We didn't have too many forms of recreation, but one of the biggest was deer hunting in the fall. Though we farmers loved the sight of whitetails we also realized that they were a crop, a crop that needed to be harvested, like corn, alfalfa, and potatoes. Because of the crop damage deer can inflict we knew that their numbers needed to be controlled and kept in balance

Unfortunately, in too many parts of America automobiles harvest the whitetail population. In 1994, 42,624 whitetails were killed on Pennsylvania highways. This is not the way to steward a resource as magnificent as the whitetail.

Whitetails are prolific breeders. When they are left unchecked their numbers quickly get out of balance with the range's carrying capacity. The end result is that all nature suffers because of habitat destruction.

with the land's carrying capacity. To us this philosophy was a basic premise of being good stewards of the land. Unfortunately this idea began to change as America moved from an agrarian to an urban society.

Today white-tailed deer management is very controversial in this country. On the one side are the hunters who have harvested the excess deer for decades. On the other side are the anti-hunter/animal rights groups who wish to outlaw all forms of hunting in America. For several years I was a nature photography instructor for the National Wildlife Federation at different summits they conducted each summer. During my lectures I would always tell my class that my photography was an outgrowth of being a hunter. Needless to say this generated many pleasant debates from classmates. On one occasion I even had a student say, "Charlie, you are an enigma to me. How can you take such beautiful pictures of wildlife and then turn around and hunt?"

For the better part of an hour I explained to this person that I was brought up on a farm, learned to hunt at a very early age, and viewed hunting as a heritage and true form of stewardship. I also explained that I enjoy eating meat—especially wild turkey and whitetail—and that my family grows a large garden. The garden, coupled with hunting, makes us pretty much self-sufficient when it comes to food. That made sense to this individual, but what she viewed as "sport hunting" did not. There's no question that hunting and the part it plays in the future of the white-tailed deer is a key issue as we look to the year 2000 and beyond.

Despite all the arguments, only one method of controlling whitetail populations survives scrutiny. Only by the controlled harvesting through hunting of both bucks and does will deer numbers be kept in balance with the range's carrying capacity.

The next century holds many unanswered questions concerning the whitetail. This scene of New York's Adirondack Mountains was one of the strongholds for the whitetail when deer populations plummeted in the late 1800s. With proper planning it can continue to be a stronghold into the future.

It's safe to say that the whitetail has played a big part in the successes I've seen. For this reason I treat it with a great deal of respect. And this respect means that I try very hard to make sure that it is not abused. Though this may seem contradictory, in that I'm a hunter, I also realize that there is a very ugly side to the whitetail world. This takes place when politics and sound management get in the way of keeping a deer herd in balance with its range's carrying capacity.

Unfortunately, the majority of people see whitetailed deer during the summer and autumn months when vegetation is lush and abundant and deer are in their prime physical condition. When winter arrives and things become stressful, however, man is nowhere around. Because non-hunters seldom see the stress and struggle side of the whitetail they don't understand why deer numbers have to be reduced. Therefore, as we look to the next century all whitetail enthusiasts need to think of a deer herd in terms of what's available for them to eat during the winter months, and manage their numbers accordingly. This is one of the tenets of being good stewards of what God has entrusted to us.

One of the great wildlife challenges for all Americans in the next century is managing our exploding whitetail populations. On paper it looks easy enough but in reality it can be a mon-

A porcupine recycles the antlers of a white-tailed buck.

umental task. As mentioned in the first chapter, white-tailed deer are very prolific. How prolific? Let me illustrate. The George Reserve is a 1,146 acre high-fenced enclosure in southern Michigan. In 1928 six adult whitetails were introduced to it, and in seven short years the protected population had grown to 222 animals. Make no mistake, whitetail populations can increase and get out of hand quickly if they are not controlled. To carry this one step further, when you realize that a whitetail's range is very small and he needs approximately one ton of food a year to survive, it quickly becomes apparent how rapidly habitat can be destroyed.

Unfortunately, what took place on the George Reserve is happening all over America. With shopping plazas and housing developments gobbling up land at a record pace, white-tailed deer are becoming highly visible as they attempt to find suitable food sources. With limited habitat and no place to go, deer often become a nuisance throughout the year, especially during winter months when they begin feeding on ornamental shrubs and trees around houses. And in some locations habitat destruction is so severe from whitetail over-browsing that starvation takes place. Few realize it, but when whitetails destroy a forest's habitat more than just deer suffer. Whole species of plants disappear along with the nesting sites of many songbirds. So, if they are not controlled, whitetails can quickly create a negative domino effect in nature.

Biologists across America realize this and attempt to manage whitetail numbers accordingly. But sadly their hands are often tied by our political process. Instead of letting biologists steward America's deer herds through hunting,

politicians, with their ears and careers to the wind, often react to anti-hunting demagogy and emotion rather than proven science. As a result the mismanagement of the white-tailed deer is becoming more and more a political chess match between the animal rights movement and biologists. This is evidenced by the growing number of areas being put off-limits to hunting. An example of this is occurring in Durand Eastman Park of Rochester, New York. Rather than let hunters harvest the park's exploding whitetail population, animal rights organizations have forced authorities to have "sharp-shooters" thin the herd. With all the regulations involved, it's costing taxpayers around $400 to remove each deer. This mentality is as far from being stewardship as the east is from the west.

As a nature photographer and hunter whose roots are on the farm I've sat back and observed the hunting/anti-hunting debate for years. Aside from it getting uglier by the year it's apparent that common sense is grossly lacking from both sides in this debate. The end result is that the whitetail is becoming the big loser. As we head into the next century, we need to come to grips with the fact that white-tailed deer are not people but rather a valuable renewable resource. We also need to realize that without the hunter/sportsman the wildlife populations in this country would not be what they are today. Since 1937 America's sportsmen (through the Pittman-Robertson Act) have provided over 1.5 billion dollars to the restoration and preservation of our wildlife. During the same period the amount of money provided by the anti-hunting community has been minimal. Through self-imposed taxes on firearms and ammunition, sportsmen will be contributing 148 million dollars

to wildlife and conservation in the United States during fiscal 1996. This isn't chicken feed, and the anti-hunting groups would be wise to begin doing the same if they truly love wildlife, as they say they do. The special side of this sportsmen's movement is that all wildlife, from songbirds to whitetails, has benefited.

During the last few years the anti-hunting movement has tried to come up with alternatives to hunting. Frankly, I believe a reality check is in order. To date, alternatives like sterilization, trap and transfer and specialized hunts by "snipers" has not worked, not to mention being far too costly. What really scares me as a lover of nature is any group who tries to eliminate proven management methods before a sound alternative is found. This kind of mentality is rampant in wildlife circles today and only compounds the problems wildlife managers face.

On the other side of the coin, I believe that the hunter must present a better impression to the non-hunting population. True, hunters have "put their money where their mouth is." But unfortunately a few bad apples have tarnished some great accomplishments. Looking to the future, I believe the hunter must strive to better educate the public about why whitetails must be managed. They also need to come to grips with the fact that hunting is not a right but rather a privilege. Also, there needs to be a de-emphasis on the big antler movement that is so prevalent in this country. The whole issue of records and record-book bucks has given hunting a bad name. I'm a strong advocate of having a quality white-tailed deer herd. And with quality comes bucks with big antlers. But I draw the line when antler size fogs the real reason for hunting.

For me, hunting is more than big antlers or shallow words. It's amber sunrises and the smell of leaves in an October forest. It's fluffy snowflakes landing on a cold gun barrel, and the smell of wet wool at the end of a day's hunt. It's the rapid heartbeat as a white-tailed buck gracefully moves through the woods, and the *fummmp* sound of an arrow's release. It's the skinning, butchering, and cooking process of getting the deer from the woods to the table. In short, hunting is being there. It's experiencing all that nature offers.

So, where do we go from here? As goes the whitetail so goes the whole American wildlife movement. No other animal on this continent is so visible, so loved, and so valuable to millions of people as the white-tailed deer. If we as a people can come together and insure that a quality population exists then future generations of Americans will benefit greatly. But if the hunting and anti-hunting factions drift further and further apart this magnificent animal will suffer. For the whitetail to survive and thrive it will take a unique mix of teamwork from all Americans. Anything less will be unfortunate.

Index